Family Circle®

Hometown COOKING®

Volume 6
Meredith® Consumer Marketing
Des Moines, Iowa

*Family Circle*₀ **Hometown Cooking**₀

Meredith₀ Consumer Marketing
Vice President, Consumer Marketing: Janet Donnelly
Consumer Product Marketing Director: Heather Sorensen
Business Director: Ron Clingman
Consumer Marketing Product Manager: Wendy Merical
Senior Production Manager: Al Rodruck

Waterbury Publications, Inc.
Editorial Director: Lisa Kingsley
Associate Editor: Tricia Bergman
Contributing Writer: Deborah Wagman
Creative Director: Ken Carlson
Associate Design Director: Doug Samuelson
Graphic Designer: Mindy Samuelson
Contributing Copy Editors: Gretchen Kauffman, Peg Smith
Contributing Indexer: Elizabeth T. Parson

*Family Circle*₀ Magazine
Editor in Chief: Linda Fears
Creative Director: Karmen Lizzul
Food Director: Regina Ragone, M.S., R.D.
Senior Food Editor: Julie Miltenberger
Associate Food Editor: Michael Tyrrell
Assistant Food Editor: Melissa Knific
Editorial Assistant: Megan Bingham

Meredith National Media Group
President: Tom Harty

Meredith Corporation
Chairman and Chief Executive Officer: Stephen M. Lacy

In Memoriam: E.T. Meredith III (1933–2003)

Copyright © 2013 by Meredith Corporation.
Des Moines, Iowa.
First Edition.
Printed in China.
ISSN: 1940-9109
ISBN: 978-0-696-30137-7

All of us at Meredith₀ Consumer Marketing are dedicated to providing you with information and ideas to enhance your home. We welcome your comments and suggestions. Write to us at: Meredith Consumer Marketing, 1716 Locust St., Des Moines, IA 50309-3023.

Pictured on the front cover:
S'mores Ice Cream Pie
(recipe on page 180)
Photography by Jason Donnelly

Vegetable-Mango Beef Stir-Fry from the 2011 National Beef Cook-Off® funded by the Beef Checkoff. www.beefcookoff.org (page 115)

Funded by
the Beef Checkoff

Enjoy prizewinning recipes from hometown America!

The cozy club of enthusiastic cooks and bakers—those apron-clad queens and kings of the kitchen who enter recipe after recipe of painstakingly perfected dishes in the nation's recipe contests and cook-offs—are some of the brightest stars of American cuisine. Taste their recipes for yourself. This, our sixth edition of *Family Circle® Hometown Cooking®*, is packed with the year's top race winners. And their award-winning recipes are not the kind of intimidators common to cooking shows and food magazines—they're the kind of recipes that you can make in your very own kitchen.

Open this book to discover them, along with chapters chock-full of inspiration for creating not only family-friendly but also company-special dishes made with easy-to-find ingredients and clear directions for easy-to-master cooking techniques.

So dig in. From breakfasts that bring even the most reluctant sleepyheads to the table to tasty potluck portables, a treasure trove of handheld feasts, 30-minute meals, and to-die-for desserts, these are the kind of foods that your friends and family will relish.

— **The Editors**

table of
contents

CHAPTER 1
getting started

Begin the bash with this selection of dips, tidbits, and fabulous finger food.

BACON-WRAPPED, AVOCADO-
STUFFED SHRIMP ROLLS

DIPS AND SPREADS

Bacon-Cheddar Cheese Ball, 22

Frannie's Vidalia Onion
Jalapeño Surprise, 15

Hot Artichoke and Banana Pepper Dip, 17

Hot Chipped Beef Dip, 16

HOT APPETIZERS

Baby Brats in a Blanket, 12

Bacon-Wrapped, Avocado-Stuffed
Shrimp Rolls, 19

Chinese Coca-Cola Wings, 10

Gorgonzola and Pear Pizza, 9

Sage and Bacon Meatballs, 11

Sausage Bites, 12

COLD APPETIZERS

Caraway Veggies, 22

Greek Stuffed Eggs, 21

Marinated Shrimp Scampi, 24

NUTS AND SNACK MIX

Caramel Snack Mix, 25

Onion and Garlic
Macadamia Nuts, 27

Sweet and Spicy Nuts, 26

Gorgonzola and Pear Pizza

It was Peggy Linberg's dislike for tomato sauce that got her imagination churning away on this ingenious alternative. The Upland, California, resident describes her honey-drizzled fruit and cheese pizza—a recipe so easy that even her grandchildren can make it—as a "sweet, salty combination that people love." Judges of the Bay English Muffin Pizza Challenge certainly loved it—Peggy won Grand Prize, an honor that earned a trip for two to southern Italy, where she stayed in Frances Ford Coppola's villa, complete with hands-on pasta-making lessons.

MAKES 8 servings **PREP** 10 minutes **BAKE** 10 minutes at 400°F

4   **Bays English Muffins, split and lightly toasted**
3   **tablespoons olive oil**
1   **cup shredded Italian cheese blend**
⅔   **cup crumbled Gorgonzola cheese (3 ounces)**
1   **Bosc pear, cored and cut into 16 thin slices**
2   **teaspoons lemon juice**
½   **cup coarsely chopped walnuts, toasted***
     Sea salt (optional)
     Honey (optional)

1 Preheat oven to 400°F. Place toasted English muffin halves on a foil-lined baking sheet. Drizzle oil over muffins; sprinkle evenly with Italian cheese and half of the Gorgonzola cheese.

2 Coat the pear slices lightly with lemon juice; place on the cheeses. Sprinkle remaining Gorgonzola cheese and walnuts over pear slices.

3 Bake pizzas for 10 minutes or until cheese is melted. If desired, sprinkle lightly with sea salt and drizzle with honey.

***Note:** To toast nuts, seeds, or shredded coconut, spread pieces in a single layer in a shallow baking pan. Bake in a 350°F oven for 5 to 10 minutes or until pieces are golden brown, stirring once or twice.

PER SERVING 265 **CAL**; 18 g **FAT** (6 g **SAT**); 19 g **CARB**; 23 mg **CHOL**; 411 mg **SODIUM**; 2 g **FIBER**; 10 g **PRO**

Chinese Coca-Cola Wings

Cola, soy sauce, and white wine simmer up into a deliciously syrupy sauce that coats chicken wings with potent Asian flavor.

MAKES 12 servings **PREP** 25 minutes **MARINATE** 1 hour **COOK** 15 minutes

12	chicken wings (about 2½ pounds total)
1	cup Coca-Cola
¼	cup reduced-sodium soy sauce
2	tablespoons dry sherry or dry white wine
3	thin slices peeled fresh ginger
2	cloves garlic, thinly sliced
¼	teaspoon crushed red pepper
2	tablespoons vegetable oil
1	tablespoon sesame seeds, toasted (see note, page 9)

1 Cut off and discard tips of chicken wings. Cut wings at joints to form 24 pieces. Place chicken wing pieces in a resealable plastic bag set in a shallow dish.

2 For marinade, in a small bowl combine cola, soy sauce, sherry, ginger, garlic, and crushed red pepper. Pour marinade over chicken wings. Seal bag; turn to coat chicken. Marinate in the refrigerator for 1 hour, turning bag occasionally. Drain chicken wings, reserving marinade. Pat wings dry with paper towels.

3 In a large skillet heat oil over medium-high heat. Add chicken wings; cook about 10 minutes or until browned on both sides, turning occasionally to brown evenly. Drain off fat. Pour the reserved marinade over chicken wings.

4 Bring to simmering. Cook, covered, for 5 minutes. Cook, uncovered, about 10 minutes more until chicken is no longer pink and marinade is slightly thickened, turning wings once. Transfer to a serving platter. Sprinkle with sesame seeds.

PER SERVING 249 **CAL**; 18 g **FAT** (5 g **SAT**); 73 mg **CHOL**; 264 mg **SODIUM**; 3 g **CARB**; 0 g **FIBER**; 18 g **PRO**

Sage and Bacon Meatballs

Everything is better with bacon, and these magnificent meatballs are no exception.

MAKES 16 servings   **PREP** 40 minutes   **BAKE** 25 minutes at 350°F   **COOL** 15 minutes   **BROIL** 4 minutes

24 **slices bacon**
2 **eggs, lightly beaten**
2 **cups whipping cream**
1½ **cups finely chopped red onion (1 medium)**
½ **cup ground toasted pecans or almonds
   (see note, page 9)**
6 **tablespoons snipped fresh sage**
¼ **teaspoon salt**
¼ **teaspoon black pepper**
2 **pounds ground pork**
2 **cloves garlic, minced**
   Fresh sage leaves (optional)

1 Preheat oven to 350°F. In a large skillet cook 8 slices of the bacon on medium heat until crisp; drain on paper towels. Cook remaining bacon for 4 to 5 minutes or just until beginning to brown, turning once. Drain on paper towels. Reserve 2 tablespoons drippings in skillet. Finely chop the crisp bacon; set aside.

2 In a large bowl combine eggs, ¼ cup of the whipping cream, 1 cup of the red onion, pecans, ¼ cup of the fresh sage, salt, and pepper. Add pork and three-fourths of the finely chopped bacon; mix well.

3 Shape into 32 meatballs. Place meatballs in a single layer in a roasting pan. Bake, uncovered, about 25 minutes or until done (160°F). Cool 15 minutes.

4 Thread 2 meatballs and 1 slice of the partially cooked bacon onto a 4-inch skewer, weaving bacon around meatballs. Repeat with remaining meatballs and bacon slices. Place on the unheated rack of a broiler pan. Broil 3 to 4 inches from the heat for 4 to 5 minutes or until bacon is crisp, turning once.

5 Meanwhile for sauce cook the remaining ½ cup onion and the garlic on medium heat in the reserved drippings for 2 to 3 minutes or until tender. Stir in the remaining whipping cream and the remaining snipped sage. Bring to boiling; reduce heat. Simmer for 5 minutes or until thickened. Stir in the remaining finely chopped bacon.

6 Arrange meatball kabobs on a platter. If desired, garnish with sage leaves. Serve with sauce.

PER SERVING 370 **CAL**; 33 g **FAT** (14 g **SAT**); 123 mg **CHOL**;
369 mg **SODIUM**; 3 g **CARB**; 1 g **FIBER**; 16 g **PRO**

Sausage Bites

These quick and easy appetizers combine sweet, savory, zingy, and smoky flavors all in one bite, making them a popular pick at any event.

MAKES 20 servings **START TO FINISH** 30 minutes

- 1½ **cups barbecue sauce**
- ⅔ **cup orange marmalade**
- ½ **teaspoon dry mustard**
- ⅛ **teaspoon ground allspice**
- 12 **ounces cooked bratwurst, cut into ½-inch slices**
- 12 **ounces cooked kielbasa, cut diagonally into ½-inch slices**
- 8 **ounces small cooked smoked sausage links**

1 In a large saucepan combine barbecue sauce, marmalade, dry mustard, and allspice. Cook and stir over medium-high heat until bubbly.

2 Stir in bratwurst, kielbasa, and smoked sausage links. Cook, covered, over medium-low heat about 20 minutes or until heated through, stirring occasionally.

PER SERVING 206 **CAL**; 13 g **FAT** (5 g **SAT**); 27 mg **CHOL**; 609 mg **SODIUM**; 16 g **CARB**; 0 g **FIBER**; 6 g **PRO**

Slow Cooker Directions: In a 3½- or 4-quart slow cooker combine barbecue sauce, marmalade, dry mustard, and allspice. Stir in bratwurst, kielbasa, and smoked sausage links. Cover and cook on high-heat setting for 2½ to 3 hours. Serve immediately or keep warm, covered, on low-heat setting for up to 2 hours.

Baby Brats in a Blanket

Consider doubling this recipe—these plump little morsels will disappear quickly. Another time, make them for dinner, skipping the slicing step and serving them whole. They'll be a big hit with your kids.

MAKES 16 servings **PREP** 30 minutes
BAKE 15 minutes at 400°F

- 8 **cooked smoked bratwurst**
- ½ **cup pickle relish, well drained**
- ½ **cup sauerkraut, rinsed, well drained, and chopped**
- 2 **11-ounce packages refrigerated breadsticks (12 each)**
- 8 **slices cheddar or American cheese, halved lengthwise**
  Homemade Ketchup (optional)

1 Preheat oven to 400°F. Grease a large baking sheet; set aside. Make a ½-inch-deep slit in each bratwurst by cutting lengthwise down the center almost to the ends. Using a spoon, remove some of the meat from slits. Spoon 1 tablespoon of the relish and 1 tablespoon of the sauerkraut into each slit, packing gently.

2 Unroll breadsticks. Using three of the breadsticks, wrap each stuffed bratwurst in a spiral fashion, covering most of the bratwurst except the very ends. Place wrapped bratwurst, stuffing sides up, on the prepared baking sheet.

3 Bake for 15 to 17 minutes or until bratwurst are heated through and dough is puffed and browned, topping with cheese for the last 5 minutes of baking.

4 Using a serrated knife, cut each bratwurst into four pieces. If desired, serve with Homemade Ketchup.

PER SERVING 303 **CAL**; 19 g **FAT** (8 g **SAT**); 40 mg **CHOL**; 824 mg **SODIUM**; 23 g **CARB**; 1 g **FIBER**; 12 g **PRO**

Homemade Ketchup: In a medium saucepan combine one 28-ounce can undrained diced fire-roasted tomatoes, ½ cup finely chopped onion (1 medium), ¼ cup packed brown sugar, ¼ cup cider vinegar, 2 tablespoons olive oil, 2 tablespoons tomato paste, 1 teaspoon garlic powder, and ⅛ teaspoon allspice. Bring to boiling; reduce heat. Simmer, uncovered, about 45 minutes or until liquid is nearly evaporated. If desired, use a potato masher to break up the tomato pieces.

BABY BRATS IN A BLANKET

Frannie's Vidalia Onion Jalapeño Surprise

Georgian Fran Pittman entered the 2012 Sweet Vidalia Onion Festival's recipe contest simply to help out a friend who was trying to gather new entrants for the event. Her kindness paid off—her adaptation of a common local dish consisting of onions, mayonnaise, and Swiss cheese took first prize in the Appetizer category, winning $100, but her jalapeño-spiked version won Overall honors and a beautiful pewter onion as well.

MAKES 28 servings **PREP** 20 minutes **BAKE** 30 minutes at 375°F

2   **8-ounce packages shredded Mexican-style four-cheese blend**
4   **cups coarsely chopped Vidalia onions (4 medium)**
1   **8-ounce package cream cheese, softened and cut up**
1   **cup mayonnaise**
2   **jalapeños, chopped***
2   **teaspoons Old Bay seasoning**
2   **teaspoons Texas Pete hot sauce**
1   **teaspoon garlic salt**
½   **teaspoon black pepper**
1½ **cups crushed Ritz crackers (1 sleeve, about 35 crackers)**
    Butter-flavor nonstick cooking spray
3   **slices bacon, crisp-cooked and crumbled**
½   **cup Captain Rodney's Boucan Glaze**
    Ritz crackers
    Texas Pete hot sauce

1 Preheat oven to 375°F. In a large bowl combine Mexican cheese, onions, cream cheese, mayonnaise, jalapeños, seasoning, 2 teaspoons hot sauce, the garlic salt, and black pepper. Mix well and spoon into a 2-quart baking dish, spreading evenly. Top cheese mixture with 1½ cups crushed crackers. Lightly coat with nonstick spray.

2 Bake, uncovered, for 30 minutes or until hot and bubbly. Remove from oven and top with bacon. Drizzle with Boucan glaze.

3 Serve with crackers and additional hot sauce.

***Note:** Because hot chile peppers, such as jalapeños, contain volatile oils that can burn your skin and eyes, avoid direct contact with then as much as possible. When working with chile peppers, wear plastic or rubber gloves. If your bare hands touch the chile peppers, wash your hands well with soap and water.

PER SERVING 177 **CAL**; 14 g **FAT** (6 g **SAT**); 28 mg **CHOL**; 323 mg **SODIUM**; 7 g **CARB**; 1 g **FIBER**; 5 g **PRO**;

Hot Chipped Beef Dip

Retro appetizers—such as this dip born in the '60s—are making a big comeback on the cocktail circuit. The slow cooker version allows you plenty of time for last-minute party preparations.

MAKES 28 servings **PREP** 15 minutes **BAKE** 20 minutes at 400°F

- 1 **8-ounce package cream cheese, softened**
- 1 **8-ounce carton sour cream**
- ¼ **cup milk**
- 1 **tablespoon cream-style prepared horseradish**
- 1 **teaspoon Worcestershire sauce**
- 2 **2.5-ounce packages sliced dried beef, coarsely chopped**
- ½ **cup finely chopped red onion (1 small)**
- ½ **cup finely chopped celery (1 stalk)**
- 2 **teaspoons snipped fresh dillweed or ½ teaspoon dried dillweed**
  Sliced dill pickles (optional)
  Cornichons, potato chips, and/or crisp rye crackers

1 Preheat oven to 400°F. In a medium mixing bowl beat cream cheese until fluffy. Beat in sour cream, milk, horseradish, and Worcestershire sauce until combined. Stir in dried beef, onion, celery, and dill. Transfer mixture to a seasoned or generously greased 8- to 9-inch cast-iron skillet or oven-safe casserole.

2 Bake about 20 minutes or until bubbly. If desired, top with dill pickles. Serve with cornichons, potato chips, and/or rye crackers.

PER SERVING 56 **CAL**; 5 g **FAT** (3 g **SAT**); 17 mg **CHOL**; 182 mg **SODIUM**; 1 g **CARB**; 0 g **FIBER**; 2 g **PRO**

Slow Cooker Directions: Prepare dip as directed, then transfer dip to a 1½-quart slow cooker. Cover and cook on low-heat setting for 3 hours or until heated through (if no heat setting is available, cook for 2 hours). Stir before serving. If desired, top with dill pickles. Serve as directed.

Hot Artichoke and Banana Pepper Dip

Do splurge on freshly grated Parmesan cheese when you make this creamy dip—the flavor is outstanding.

MAKES 32 servings **PREP** 25 minutes **BAKE** 25 minutes at 400°F

- **6** **9-ounce packages frozen artichoke hearts, cooked, drained, and coarsely chopped**
- **1** **cup finely chopped yellow, red, or green sweet pepper**
- **16** **ounces Parmigiano-Reggiano or Parmesan cheese, finely shredded**
- **2** **cups light mayonnaise**
- **1** **medium banana pepper, seeded and cut into rings**
- **2** **tablespoons chopped fresh garlic**
- **4** **teaspoons ground cumin**
  Crackers

1 Preheat oven to 400°F. In a large bowl mix together artichoke hearts, sweet pepper, cheese, mayonnaise, banana pepper, garlic, and cumin. Transfer mixture to a 3-quart rectangular or oval baking dish.

2 Bake, uncovered, for 25 to 30 minutes or until top is golden brown and mixture is hot throughout. Serve with crackers.

PER SERVING 101 **CAL**; 8 g **FAT** (2 g **SAT**); 11 mg **CHOL**; 251 mg **SODIUM**; 5 g **CARB**; 2 g **FIBER**; 4 g **PRO**

Bacon-Wrapped, Avocado-Stuffed Shrimp Rolls

Although Acworth, Georgia, resident Dee Guelcher has been active in the cooking contest culture—a community that she describes as "extremely supportive" rather than the "do-or-die battle" she expected—for a mere 3 years, she has created an impressive number of prize-winning recipes in that time. Her submission to the 2012 Hass Avocado cooking contest—an appetizer of avocado-stuffed, bacon-wrapped shrimp dolled up even further with an avocado-mustard dipping sauce—earned her a round trip to attend the Rose Bowl Parade in Pasadena, California.

MAKES 15 servings **PREP** 30 minutes **BAKE** 15 minutes at 350°F

1   large ripe Hass avocado, halved, seeded and peeled

1   shallot, minced

2   tablespoons chopped fresh dill

2   teaspoons salt

1   teaspoon black pepper

15 large or jumbo shrimp, peeled, deveined, and butterflied

15 slices precooked bacon

1   8-ounce can refrigerated crescent rolls or refrigerated crescent dough for recipes

1   large ripe Hass avocado, halved, seeded and peeled

2   tablespoons Dijon mustard

2   tablespoons agave nectar

1 Preheat oven to 350°F. For stuffing, in a small bowl mash one of the seeded and peeled avocados. Add shallot, 1 tablespoon of the dill, 1 teaspoon of the salt, and ½ teaspoon of the pepper.

2 With a spoon, stuff the shrimp with the avocado stuffing. Wrap one piece of bacon the around each shrimp. Seal seams of crescent rolls. Pat rolls or sheet to a 15 x 8-inch rectangle. Slice the crescent rolls crosswise into 1-inch strips and starting near one end wrap the bacon around in a spiral fashion. Place shrimp rolls on a baking sheet.

3 Bake for 15 minutes or until bacon is crisp and shrimp are opaque.

4 Meanwhile, for the dipping sauce, place the remaining seeded and peeled avocado in a food processor. Add mustard, agave nectar, remaining dill, salt, and pepper. Cover and process until smooth. Serve with warm shrimp rolls.

PER SERVING 137 **CAL**; 8 g **FAT** (2 g **SAT**); 5 g **PRO**; 10 g **CARB**; 1 g **FIBER**; 675 mg **SODIUM**; 29 mg **CHOL**

Greek Stuffed Eggs

Registered dietitian Jessica Hildebrandt—a nutritional counselor in Lancaster, Pennsylvania—seems to do her best work under pressure. Although she had experimented with her Greek Stuffed Eggs recipe before, it was not until an hour before deadline that she perfected her recipe, snapped a quick photo, and sent in her entry. For her quick thinking and healthful recipe, Jessica took Grand Prize in Eggland's Best 2011 contest—and was awarded an all-expenses-paid trip to the Food and Nutrition Conference and Expo in San Diego.

MAKES 12 servings **START TO FINISH** 25 minutes

6	hard-cooked* Eggland's Best eggs
2	tablespoons low-fat Greek yogurt
1½	tablespoons freshly squeezed lemon juice
2	teaspoons extra virgin olive oil
⅛	teaspoon salt
	Dash freshly ground black pepper
¼	cup finely chopped onion
¼	cup finely chopped cucumber
¼	cup crumbled feta cheese
2	tablespoons snipped fresh oregano
	Oregano leaves

1 Halve hard-cooked eggs lengthwise and remove yolks. Set whites aside. Place yolks in a medium bowl; mash with a fork. Add yogurt, lemon juice, olive oil, salt, and pepper; mix until smooth. Add onion, cucumber, feta, and 2 tablespoons snipped oregano; mix well.

2 Stuff egg white halves. Garnish with oregano leaves.

*Hard-Cooked Eggs: Place 6 eggs in a single layer in a large saucepan (do not stack eggs). Add enough cold water to cover the eggs by 1 inch. Bring to a rapid boil over high heat. Remove from heat, cover, and let stand for 15 minutes; drain. Run cold water over the eggs or place them in ice water until cool enough to handle; drain. To peel eggs, gently tap each egg on the countertop. Roll the egg between the palms of your hands. Peel off eggshell, starting at the large end.

PER SERVING 58 **CAL**; 4 g **FAT** (1 g **SAT**); 96 mg **CHOL**; 91 mg **SODIUM**; 1 g **CARB**; 0 g **FIBER**; 4 g **PRO**

Bacon-Cheddar Cheese Ball

Cheese balls fell from fashion for a few decades, but in recent years they have emerged as a chic and stylish party provision.

MAKES 4 servings **PREP** 40 minutes
STAND 45 minutes **CHILL** 2 hours

- 8 ounces extra-sharp cheddar cheese,* finely shredded (2 cups)
- 1 8-ounce package reduced-fat cream cheese (Neufchâtel)
- ½ of a 2-ounce jar sliced pimiento, rinsed, drained, patted dry, and chopped
- 2 tablespoons apricot preserves
- 1 tablespoon milk
- 1½ teaspoons Worcestershire sauce
- ⅛ teaspoon bottled hot pepper sauce
- 15 slices bacon, crisp-cooked and drained
- ¼ cup pistachio nuts, chopped
  Celery sticks, cucumber slices, apricot halves, crackers, and/or toasted baguette-style French bread slices

1 In a large mixing bowl let cheddar cheese and cream cheese stand at room temperature for 30 minutes. Add pimiento, preserves, milk, Worcestershire sauce, and hot pepper sauce. Crumble 10 of the bacon slices and add to mixture. Beat with an electric mixer on medium until almost smooth.

2 Crumble the remaining 5 bacon slices. Separately cover and chill cheese mixture and the crumbled bacon for 2 to 24 hours.

3 Shape cheese mixture into a ball; roll in crumbled bacon and chopped pistachios. Let stand for 15 minutes. Serve with celery, cucumber, apricots, crackers, and/or toasted bread.

***Note:** For a cheese ball, it works better to shred the cheese yourself than to buy shredded cheese.

PER SERVING 218 **CAL**; 17 g **FAT** (9 g **SAT**); 49 mg **CHOL**; 361 mg **SODIUM**; 6 g **CARB**; 1 g **FIBER**; 11 g **PRO**

Caraway Veggies

Health-conscious guests will appreciate finding a low-fat, high-flavor option like this on the buffet table.

MAKES 12 servings **PREP** 45 minutes **CHILL** 2 hours

- 1½ small carrots with tops, trimmed and peeled
- 6 cups cauliflower florets
- 2 medium red and/or green sweet peppers, cut into wedges
- ¾ cup olive oil
- 1 tablespoon caraway seeds, crushed
- 1 cup white wine vinegar
- ½ teaspoon salt
- ½ teaspoon crushed red pepper

1 In a medium saucepan cook carrots, covered, in a small amount of boiling water for 3 to 5 minutes or until crisp-tender. Drain; rinse with cold water. Drain well. In a large saucepan cook cauliflower, covered, in a small amount of boiling water about 3 minutes or until crisp-tender. Drain; rinse with cold water. Drain well. Place carrots, cauliflower, and sweet peppers in separate resealable plastic bags.

2 For marinade, in a medium saucepan combine oil and caraway seeds. Cook and stir over low heat for 4 to 5 minutes or until oil is warm and slightly fragrant; cool slightly. In a large glass measure whisk together the oil mixture, vinegar, salt, and crushed red pepper.

3 Pour about ½ cup of the marinade over the carrots, about 1 cup of the marinade over the cauliflower, and the remaining marinade over the sweet peppers. Seal bags; turn to coat. Chill for 2 to 6 hours, turning bags often.

4 To serve, drain vegetables, discarding marinade. Arrange vegetables on a serving platter.

PER SERVING 52 **CAL**; 3 g **FAT** (0 g **SAT**); 0 mg **CHOL**; 143 mg **SODIUM**; 5 g **CARB**; 1 g **FIBER**; 2 g **PRO**

CARAWAY VEGGIES

Marinated Shrimp Scampi

Be mindful not to marinate shrimp for longer than one hour—doing so may cause the delicate crustaceans to become tough.

MAKES 10 to 12 servings **PREP** 35 minutes **MARINATE** 1 hour **BROIL** 4 minutes

- ¼ **cup olive oil**
- ¼ **cup dry white wine**
- 6 **garlic, minced**
- 2 **teaspoons finely shredded lemon peel**
- ½ **teaspoon salt**
- ½ **teaspoon crushed red pepper**
- 2 **pounds fresh or frozen extra-jumbo shrimp in shells (32 to 40)**
- 2 **tablespoons fresh parsley**
  Lemon slices

1 For marinade, in a small bowl combine olive oil, wine, garlic, lemon peel, salt, and crushed red pepper.

2 Thaw shrimp, if frozen. Peel and devein shrimp, leaving tails intact. Rinse shrimp; pat dry with paper towels. Place shrimp in a large resealable plastic bag set in a shallow bowl. Pour marinade over shrimp. Seal bag; turn to coat shrimp. Marinate in the refrigerator for 1 hour.

3 Preheat broiler. Remove shrimp from marinade, reserving marinade. Arrange shrimp on the unheated rack of a broiler pan. Broil 4 to 5 inches from heat for 2 minutes. Turn shrimp over and brush with reserved marinade; discard any remaining marinade. Broil for 2 to 4 minutes more or until shrimp are opaque.

4. Mound shrimp on a serving platter; sprinkle with parsley. Served with lemon wedges.

PER SERVING 126 **CAL**; 4 g **FAT** (1 g **SAT**); 138 mg **CHOL**; 193 mg **SODIUM**; 2 g **CARB**; 1 g **FIBER**; 19 g **PRO**

Caramel Snack Mix

This crunchy concoction is perfect for parties, a terrific tailgating tote-along, or kid-pleasing after-school snack. In a small bag tied with a pretty ribbon, it's a welcome hostess gift.

MAKES 30 servings **PREP** 15 minutes **BAKE** 30 minutes at 300°F **COOL** 30 minutes

1 **12-ounce box crispy corn and rice cereal**

1½ **cups mixed nuts, cashews, or almonds**

½ **cup packed brown sugar**

½ **cup light-color corn syrup**

½ **cup butter**

2 **cups chocolate-covered raisins, chocolate-covered peanuts, or semisweet or milk chocolate pieces**

1 Preheat oven to 300°F. In a large roasting pan combine cereal and mixed nuts; set aside.

2 In a saucepan combine brown sugar, corn syrup, and butter. Cook and stir over medium heat until butter is melted and mixture is smooth. Pour over cereal mixture; stir gently to coat.

3 Bake, uncovered, for 30 minutes, stirring twice. Remove from oven. Spread mixture on a large piece of buttered foil; cool for 30 minutes. Break into pieces. Stir in chocolate-covered raisins. Store in an airtight container up to 3 days or freeze up to 1 month.

PER SERVING 186 **CAL**; 9 g **FAT** (4 g **SAT**); 9 mg **CHOL**; 122 mg **SODIUM**; 27 g **CARB**; 1 g **FIBER**; 2 g **PRO**

Sweet and Spicy Nuts

When making these sensational snacking nuts, feel free to mix and match nut varieties in any proportion that you like—or even consider making them with just your very favorite nut.

MAKES 12 servings **PREP** 10 minutes **BAKE** 35 minutes at 300°F

- 1 **egg white**
- 1 **tablespoon water**
- 1 **pound raw whole cashews, whole almonds, walnut halves, and/or pecan halves (about 4 cups)**
- ⅓ **cup sugar**
- 2 **teaspoons salt**
- 1½ **teaspoons ground cumin**
- 1 **teaspoon paprika**
- 1 **teaspoon ground coriander**
- ½ **teaspoon cayenne pepper**
- ¼ **teaspoon ground ginger**

1 Preheat oven to 300°F. In a medium bowl beat egg white and water until frothy. Add nuts and toss to coat. Transfer to a wire-mesh sieve; drain nuts for 5 minutes.

2 Meanwhile, in a large plastic bag combine the sugar, salt, cumin, paprika, coriander, cayenne pepper, and ginger. Add the nuts; shake well to coat with the spice mixture. Spread nuts evenly in an ungreased 15 x 10 x 1-inch baking pan.

3 Bake for 35 to 40 minutes until nuts are toasted and spice mixture is dry, stirring every 10 minutes. Remove from oven; transfer to a sheet of foil. Cool completely. Break nuts apart.

PER SERVING 242 **CAL**; 18 g **FAT** (3 g **SAT**); 0 mg **CHOL**; 399 mg **SODIUM**; 18 g **CARB**; 1 g **FIBER**; 6 g **PRO**

Onion and Garlic Macadamia Nuts

Buttery-rich macadamias—completely irresistible on their own—become even more addictive when bathed in the flavors of onion and garlic. Should you be lucky enough to have leftovers, be sure to store them, tightly sealed, in the refrigerator.

MAKES 12 servings **PREP** 10 minutes **COOK** 5 minutes

3 **tablespoons olive oil**
1 **tablespoon dried parsley flakes**
1 **tablespoon onion salt**
1½ **teaspoons sugar**
1½ **teaspoons lemon juice**
¾ **teaspoon garlic powder**
3 **cups macadamia nuts (about 14 ounces)**

1 In a large skillet heat oil over medium heat for 1 to 2 minutes or until very hot. Carefully add parsley, onion salt, sugar, lemon juice, and garlic powder, stirring until combined. Add macadamia nuts.

2 Cook and stir for 5 minutes. Drain nuts on paper towels; cool.

PER SERVING 274 **CAL**; 29 g **FAT** (5 g **SAT**); 0 mg **CHOL**; 402 mg **SODIUM**; 5 g **CARB**; 3 g **FIBER**; 3 g **PRO**

CHAPTER 2
bring on breakfast

Wake up on the right side of the bed with these breakfast and brunch ideas.

OOEY-GOOEY MONKEY BREAD

Greek-Style Frittata

If the thought of filling, flipping, folding, and sliding an omelet out of the skillet presents a bigger challenge than you wish to take on, frittatas—or oven-baked, open-face omelets—are made for you.

MAKES 4 servings **PREP** 15 minutes **BAKE** 10 minutes at 425°F

½   **cup dried tomato slices (not oil-packed)**
½   **cup boiling water**
8   **eggs**
½   **cup roasted red peppers, drained and chopped**
½   **cup purchased Italian olive antipasto marinated in garlic and herbs**
1   **teaspoon dried oregano, crushed, or 2 teaspoons fresh oregano**
1   **tablespoon olive oil**
2   **ounces feta cheese, crumbled**
    Freshly ground black pepper
    Fresh oregano (optional)

1 Preheat oven to 425°F. In a small bowl combine tomatoes and ½ cup boiling water; set aside for 5 minutes. Drain tomatoes, reserving liquid.

2 Meanwhile, in a large bowl whisk eggs; stir in roasted peppers. Lightly drain and chop the antipasto mixture; add to eggs. Whisk in oregano and the reserved liquid from soaking tomatoes.

3 In a large oven-safe skillet heat oil over medium heat. Pour egg mixture into the hot skillet. Stir in feta; top with tomatoes and place in oven. Bake for 10 to 13 minutes or until set.

4 Remove from oven; cool several minutes on wire rack before serving. Top with black pepper and, if desired, fresh oregano.

PER SERVING 252 **CAL**; 18 g **FAT** (6 g **SAT**); 436 mg **CHOL**; 668 mg **SODIUM**; 7 g **CARB**; 1 g **FIBER**; 16 g **PRO**

Black Bean and Corn Breakfast Burritos

When kids grow weary of cold cereal breakfasts, surprise them with breakfast burritos. These better-for-you burritos tune right in to the Mexican flavors that children love and send them off to school both deliciously and nutritiously.

MAKES 6 servings **START TO FINISH** 30 minutes

- 2 **teaspoons olive oil**
- 2 **medium poblano chiles, seeded and chopped (see note, page 15)**
- ¾ **cup canned black beans, rinsed and drained**
- ¾ **cup frozen whole kernel corn, thawed**
- ⅓ **cup red or green salsa**
- ½ **teaspoon ground cumin**
- ½ **teaspoon chili powder**
- 6 **eggs**
   Dash salt
   Dash black pepper
- 6 **8-inch whole grain flour tortillas, warmed according to package directions**
- ¾ **cup crumbled queso fresco or shredded reduced-fat Monterey Jack cheese (3 ounces)**
- ¼ **cup snipped fresh cilantro**
- ½ **cup red or green salsa (optional)**

1 In a large skillet heat 1 teaspoon of the oil over medium heat. Add poblanos; cook about 3 minutes or just until tender, stirring occasionally. Stir in beans, corn, ⅓ cup salsa, cumin, and chili powder. Cook and stir about 2 minutes or until heated through. Remove vegetable mixture from skillet.

2 In a medium bowl combine eggs, salt, and black pepper. In the same skillet heat the remaining 1 teaspoon oil over medium heat. Pour in egg mixture. Cook, without stirring, until mixture begins to set on the bottom and around the edges. Using a spatula or a large spoon, lift and fold the partially cooked egg mixture so the uncooked portion flows underneath. Continue cooking over medium heat for 2 to 3 minutes or until mixture is cooked through but still glossy and moist. Immediately remove from heat. Gently fold in vegetable mixture.

3 Spoon about ⅔ cup of the egg mixture onto lower half each tortilla. Top with cheese and cilantro. Fold tortilla over filling. Fold in opposite sides; roll up. Cut in half to serve. If desired, serve with ½ cup salsa.

PER SERVING 297 **CAL**; 12 g **FAT** (4 g **SAT**); 216 mg **CHOL**; 602 mg **SODIUM**; 29 g **CARB**; 12 g **FIBER**; 20 g **PRO**

Fried Egg, Avocado, and Bacon Breakfast Sandwiches

To expedite this hearty breakfast sandwich, consider opting for packaged precooked bacon. Wrap the sandwiches in waxed paper and enjoy them on your busy morning commutes.

MAKES 4 servings **START TO FINISH** 25 minutes

- **1** large ripe avocado
- **2** tablespoons light mayonnaise or salad dressing
- **1** teaspoon lemon juice
- **1** clove garlic, minced
- **2** teaspoons butter or nonstick cooking spray
- **4** eggs
  Salt (optional)
  Black pepper (optional)
- **8** slices whole wheat bread, toasted
- **4** slices cheddar cheese (optional)
- **8** slices bacon, crisp-cooked, drained, and halved crosswise

1 Halve, seed, and peel avocado. Place one avocado half in a small bowl; mash with a fork or the back of a wooden spoon. Stir in mayonnaise, lemon juice, and garlic. Thinly slice the remaining avocado half. Set aside.

2 In a large skillet heat butter over medium heat until melted. (Or coat a large skillet with cooking spray; heat skillet over medium heat.) Break eggs into skillet. If desired, sprinkle with salt and pepper. Reduce heat to low; cook eggs for 3 to 4 minutes or until whites are completely set and yolks start to thicken.

3 For over easy or over hard fried eggs, when whites are completely set and the yolks start to thicken, turn eggs and cook for 30 seconds more (over easy) or 1 minute more (over hard).

4 Layer 4 of the bread slices with cheese (if desired), avocado slices, bacon, and fried eggs. Spread the remaining 4 bread slices with mayonnaise mixture; place on sandwiches, spread sides down.

PER SERVING 257 **CAL**; 14 g **FAT** (2 g **SAT**); 10 mg **CHOL**; 432 mg **SODIUM**; 27 g **CARB**; 7 g **FIBER**; 9 g **PRO**

Baked Brie Strata

Triple-cream French Brie cheese imbues this breakfast strata with a rich—almost custardy—texture. Remove the cheese's powdery rind or leave it on—the decision is entirely yours and makes little difference in flavor.

MAKES 6 servings **PREP** 25 minutes **CHILL** 4 hours **BAKE** 55 minutes at 325°F **STAND** 10 minutes

2	cups zucchini cut into ¼-inch slices
6	cups crusty sourdough bread torn into bite-size pieces (6 ounces)
1	4.4-ounce package Brie cheese
1	cup halved grape or cherry tomatoes
4	eggs, lightly beaten, or 1 cup refrigerated or frozen egg product, thawed
⅔	cup evaporated milk
⅓	cup sliced green onions
3	tablespoons snipped fresh dill
½	teaspoon salt
⅛	teaspoon black pepper

1 In a medium-size covered saucepan cook zucchini in a small amount of boiling, lightly salted water for 2 to 3 minutes or just until tender; drain.

2 Grease a 2-quart rectangular baking dish. Spread 4 cups of the bread pieces in the prepared baking dish. If desired, remove and discard rind from cheese. Cut cheese into ½-inch pieces; sprinkle evenly over bread in baking dish. Top with zucchini and tomatoes. Sprinkle with the remaining 2 cups bread pieces.

3 In a medium bowl combine eggs, evaporated milk, green onions, dill, salt, and pepper. Pour evenly over layers in dish. Press down gently with the back of a large spoon to moisten all ingredients. Cover with plastic wrap and chill for 4 to 24 hours.

4 Preheat oven to 325°F. Remove plastic wrap; cover dish with foil. Bake for 30 minutes. Uncover and bake for 25 to 30 minutes more or until a knife inserted near center comes out clean. Let stand for 10 minutes before serving.

PER SERVING 251 **CAL**; 12 g **FAT** (6 g **SAT**); 170 mg **CHOL**; 592 mg **SODIUM**; 22 g **CARB**; 2 g **FIBER**; 15 g **PRO**

Poblano-Chorizo Strata

Queso fresco—a fresh, mild-flavor skimmed milk cheese popular in Latin cooking—will not melt like the more typical cheddar, Swiss, and mozzarella cheeses do. Instead, it softens slightly and caramelizes beautifully.

MAKES 10 to 12 servings   **PREP** 40 minutes   **CHILL** 2 hours   **BAKE** 60 minutes at 325°F   **STAND** 10 minutes

½   **pound uncooked chorizo sausage**

2   **onions, thinly sliced**

2   **fresh poblano chiles, seeded and thinly sliced (see note, page 15)**

1   **red sweet pepper, thinly sliced**

8   **cups 1-inch cubes Mexican bolillo rolls or crusty Italian bread**

6   **eggs, lightly beaten**

2½ **cups milk**

1   **teaspoon Mexican oregano or regular oregano, crushed**

½   **teaspoon paprika**

½   **cup queso fresco, crumbled**
   Snipped fresh cilantro (optional)

1 In a large skillet cook chorizo over medium heat until browned. Using a slotted spoon, transfer chorizo to a bowl, reserving 1 tablespoon drippings in skillet. Add onions to drippings in skillet; cook and stir over medium heat about 10 minutes or just until tender. Stir in poblanos and sweet pepper; cook about 5 minutes or just until peppers are tender. Remove from heat. Stir in chorizo.

2 Lightly grease a 3-quart baking dish. Spread half of the bread cubes in the prepared dish. Spoon half of the chorizo mixture over. Repeat layers.

3 In a large bowl whisk together eggs, milk, oregano, and paprika. Pour evenly over layers in baking dish. Cover with foil. Chill for at least 2 hours or up to 24 hours.

4 Preheat oven to 325°F. Bake, covered, for 30 minutes. Uncover. Bake for 30 to 45 minutes more or until an instant-read thermometer inserted in the center registers 170°F. Sprinkle with cheese during last 5 minutes of baking. Let stand for 10 minutes before serving. If desired, sprinkle with cilantro.

PER SERVING 257 **CAL**; 14 g **FAT** (6 g **SAT**); 156 mg **CHOL**;
412 mg **SODIUM**; 17 g **CARB**; 1 g **FIBER**; 15 g **PRO**

Caramelized Onion and Potato Breakfast Casserole

Pancetta—a cured but unsmoked Italian pork products—comes in round slices rather than strips. Its high fat content makes it difficult to chop, but if you freeze the pancetta for 15 minutes before chopping, the process will be much easier.

MAKES 8 servings **PREP** 45 minutes **BAKE** 45 minutes at 350°F **STAND** 15 minutes

4 **cups sliced golden potatoes, cut ⅛ to ¼ inch thick (about 1 ½ pounds)**

1 **tablespoon olive oil**

2 **ounces pancetta, chopped**

3 **cups thinly sliced sweet onions, such as Vidalia or Maui**

   Butter

6 **eggs, lightly beaten**

½ **cup milk**

1 **cup shredded Gruyère cheese or Swiss cheese**

1 **teaspoon salt**

1 **teaspoon snipped fresh rosemary**

½ **teaspoon black pepper**

1 Preheat oven to 350°F. In a large saucepan cook potatoes, covered, in lightly salted boiling water about 5 minutes or until slightly tender but still firm. Drain; set aside. In a large skillet heat olive oil over medium-high heat. Add pancetta; cook until lightly browned. Using a slotted spoon, remove pancetta, reserving drippings in skillet. Set pancetta aside. Add onions to skillet. Cook and stir over medium-low heat about 20 minutes or until lightly browned and very tender. Remove from heat. Carefully stir potatoes and pancetta into onions in skillet.

2 Lightly butter a 2-quart baking dish. Spread potato mixture into prepared dish. In a medium bowl whisk together eggs and milk. Add cheese, salt, rosemary, and pepper; stir until well mixed. Pour evenly over potato mixture in baking dish.

3 Bake, uncovered, for 45 to 50 minutes or until golden and a knife inserted in the center comes out clean. Let stand for 15 minutes before serving.

PER SERVING 250 **CAL**; 13 g **FAT** (5 g **SAT**); 180 mg **CHOL**; 535 mg **SODIUM**; 22 g **CARB**; 3 g **FIBER**; 13 g **PRO**

Hash Brown-Crusted Quiche

"Impressive" most aptly describes this special breakfast dish in which golden, crispy grated potatoes form the crust for a rich and savory egg and vegetable mixture.

MAKES 8 servings **PREP** 55 minutes **BAKE** 50 minutes at 325°F **STAND** 10 minutes

1¾ **pounds russet potatoes**
½ **teaspoon salt**
⅛ **teaspoon black pepper**
1 **to 2 tablespoons olive oil**
1 **tablespoon butter**
4 **slices bacon**
1¼ **cups coarsely shredded zucchini (1 medium)**
½ **cup chopped red onion (1 medium)**
4 **eggs, lightly beaten**
1 **cup half-and-half or light cream**
¼ **teaspoon crushed red pepper**
1 **cup shredded Swiss cheese (4 ounces)**
1 **tablespoon all-purpose flour**

1 Preheat oven to 325°F. Peel and coarsely shred potatoes. Place potatoes in a large bowl; add enough water to cover potatoes. Stir well. Drain in a colander set in the sink. Repeat rinsing and draining two or three times until water runs clear. Drain, pressing out as much water as you can with a rubber spatula. Line a salad spinner with paper towels; add potatoes and spin. Repeat, if necessary, until potatoes are dry. (Or dry the potatoes by patting them dry with paper towels.) Transfer potatoes to a large bowl. Sprinkle with ¼ teaspoon of the salt and the black pepper; toss to combine.

2 In a large nonstick skillet heat 1 tablespoon of the oil and the butter over medium-high heat until butter foams. Add potatoes, spreading in an even layer. Press gently with the back of a spatula to form a potato cake. Reduce heat to medium. Cook, without stirring, about 12 minutes or until bottom is golden and crisp.

3 Place a baking sheet or cutting board over top of skillet. Carefully invert skillet to transfer potatoes to baking sheet. If necessary, add the remaining 1 tablespoon oil to skillet. Using the baking sheet, slide potatoes back into skillet. Cook about 8 minutes more or until bottom is golden.

4 Lightly grease a 9-inch pie pan or pie plate. Use the baking sheet to transfer potato cake to pie pan; press potatoes into the bottom and up the sides of the pan.

5 In a large skillet cook bacon over medium heat until crisp. Remove bacon and drain on paper towels, reserving 1 tablespoon drippings in skillet. Crumble bacon; set aside. Add zucchini and onion to the reserved drippings. Cook over medium heat for 3 to 5 minutes or until tender, stirring occasionally.

6 In a large bowl combine eggs, half-and-half, crushed red pepper, and the remaining ¼ teaspoon salt. Stir in bacon and zucchini mixture. In a small bowl toss together cheese and flour; stir into egg mixture.

7 Pour egg mixture into the potato-lined pie pan. Bake, uncovered, for 50 to 55 minutes or until a knife inserted near the center comes out clean. Let stand for 10 minutes before serving.

PER SERVING 324 **CAL**; 22 g **FAT** (9 g **SAT**); 133 mg **CHOL**; 412 mg **SODIUM**; 20 g **CARB**; 3 g **FIBER**; 12 g **PRO**

Breakfast Lasagna Rolls

Although these healthful breakfast lasagna rolls are not the sort of thing you'll make on Monday mornings, do mark this recipe for a time when you'll be entertaining overnight guests—it's an incredible treat that will let guests know how special they are.

MAKES 8 servings **PREP** 30 minutes **BAKE** 35 minutes at 350°F

8	dried whole grain lasagna noodles
	Nonstick cooking spray
8	eggs or 2 cups refrigerated or frozen egg product, thawed
2	teaspoons snipped fresh dill weed or ½ teaspoon dried dill weed
	Salt
2	teaspoons olive oil
4	cups fresh spinach
4	ounces reduced-sodium thinly sliced cooked ham
½	cup bottled roasted red sweet peppers, drained and cut into strips
1½	cups sliced fresh mushrooms
½	cup green thinly sliced onions (4)
1	12-ounce can evaporated fat-free milk
2	tablespoons flour
1	tablespoon Dijon mustard
¼	teaspoon black pepper
1	cup shredded reduced-fat cheddar cheese (4 ounces)
	Paprika

1 Preheat oven to 350°F. Cook lasagna noodles according to package directions. Drain; rinse with cold water. Drain again. Place noodles in a single layer on a sheet of foil; set aside. Lightly coat a 2-quart rectangular baking dish with cooking spray; set aside.

2 Using a whisk, in a bowl beat together eggs, dill weed, and salt. In a large nonstick skillet heat 1 teaspoon of the oil over medium heat; pour in egg mixture. Cook over medium heat, without stirring, until eggs begin to set on the bottom and around edges. With a spatula, lift and fold the partially cooked eggs so the uncooked portion flows underneath. Continue cooking over medium heat for 2 to 3 minutes or until eggs are cooked through but still glossy and moist. Remove from heat; set aside. Gently stir spinach into mixture in skillet. Cover and let stand about 3 minutes or until spinach is wilted.

3 Top each lasagna noodle with ham, cutting slices to fit noodles. Divide the egg mixture evenly on ham. Top with sweet pepper strips. Starting from a narrow end, roll up each noodle. Place the lasagna rolls, seam sides down, in the prepared baking dish; set aside.

4 For the sauce, in a large skillet heat the remaining 1 teaspoon oil over medium-high heat. Add mushrooms and green onions; cook and stir about 3 minutes or until tender. In a medium bowl stir together ¼ cup of the evaporated milk and the flour until smooth; stir in the remaining evaporated milk, the mustard, and black pepper. Stir the milk mixture into the mushroom mixture in skillet. Cook and stir until slightly thickened and bubbly. Remove from heat. Stir in the cheese until melted. Pour sauce over the lasagna rolls.

5 Cover and bake about 35 minutes or until heated through. To serve, sprinkle with paprika.

PER SERVING 287 **CAL**; 11 g **FAT** (4 g **SAT**); 229 mg **CHOL**; 437 mg **SODIUM**; 26 g **CARB**; 4 g **FIBER**; 22 g **PRO**

Mini Maple Spam Doughnuts

Jason Munson—an avionics technician for Alaska Airlines—does not give up easily. It took seven years of tinkering and recipe development for the Auburn, Washington, man to finally take First Prize for an entry in the Washington State Fair. When he did, with his recipe for crumbled Spam-topped, maple-glazed doughnuts, that was not the end of the story. His entry, praised by judges for its "taste, creativity, and presentation" went on to take Grand Prize in the Great American Spam Championship sponsored by Hormel Foods. And his reward for sticking with it? A trip for two Hawaii to attend the Spam Jam Food Festival on Waikiki Beach.

MAKES 24 servings **PREP** 25 minutes **CHILL** 1 hour **BAKE** 10 minutes at 325°F

1	**cup all-purpose flour**
3	**tablespoons packed brown sugar**
¼	**teaspoon baking soda**
⅛	**teaspoon salt**
⅓	**cup buttermilk**
1	**egg, lightly beaten**
1	**tablespoon butter, melted**
1	**12-ounce can Spam hickory smoked, Spam with bacon, or Spam classic**
¾	**cup powdered sugar**
1	**teaspoon maple flavor**
1	**tablespoon buttermilk**
	Nonstick cooking spray

1 For the batter, in large mixing bowl combine flour, brown sugar, baking soda, and salt. Stir in the ⅓ cup buttermilk, the egg, and melted butter. Beat together until well blended. Spoon batter into a pastry bag fitted with a round tip or a resealable plastic bag. Chill batter for 1 hour. Meanwhile, prepare Spam Rings and glaze.

2 For the Spam rings, remove the Spam from the can and slice from the lid side to the bottom into 12 slices (each slice about ¼ inch thick). Using a 1½-inch round biscuit cutter, cut each slice into two rounds (for a total of 24 rounds). Using a straw, knife, or small pastry tip, cut a small circle out of the center of each slice to make a ring. Place rings into a large skillet and fry until golden brown on both sides, repeating as necessary; set aside. Finely dice remaining pieces of Spam. Place the diced Spam into the same skillet and fry until golden brown; set aside.

3 For the maple glaze, in small bowl whisk together the powdered sugar, maple flavor, and the 1 tablespoon buttermilk until well combined; set aside.

4 Preheat oven to 325°F. Remove the chilled batter from the refrigerator. Lightly coat a mini doughnut pan with cooking spray. Pipe half the batter into the mini doughnut tin, filling each cup two-thirds full (if using a resealable plastic bag, snip the corner of the bag and pipe batter into the mini doughnut pan). Place half the Spam rings on top of the dough. Bake for 10 minutes or until the doughnuts spring back when touched. Allow doughnuts to cool slightly, then carefully remove from the pan. Spread maple glaze on doughnuts and top with the diced Spam. Repeat with the remaining batter and Spam rings. Serve doughnuts slightly warm.

PER SERVING 93 **CAL**; 5 g **FAT** (2 g **SAT**); 10 g **CHOL**; 231 mg **SODIUM**; 19 mg **CARB**; 0 g **FIBER**; 3 g **PRO**

Danish Fruit and Cheese Pastries

These pastry-shop perfect sweet rolls are made simple with the use of frozen sweet roll dough and ready-to-go fruit or preserves.

MAKES 24 servings **PREP** 45 minutes **RISE** 30 minutes **BAKE** 15 minutes at 350°F

2	**16-ounce loaves frozen sweet roll dough, thawed**
1	**3-ounce package cream cheese, softened**
1	**egg yolk**
2	**tablespoons sugar**
1	**tablespoon all-purpose flour**
¼	**teaspoon vanilla**
¼	**teaspoon almond extract or finely shredded orange peel**
¼	**cup any flavor jam, preserves, canned pie filling, or fruit curd**
1	**recipe Lemon Curd Icing (optional)**

1 Line two large baking sheets with parchment paper; set aside.

2 To shape spiral pastries, on a lightly floured surface roll 1 loaf of dough into a 12-inch square. Cut square into twelve 12 x 1-inch strips. With one end of a strip in each hand, twist ends in opposite directions three or four times. Coil the strip into a spiral round, tucking the outside end underneath. Repeat with remaining strips, placing 2 inches apart on baking sheets. Repeat with the remaining loaf of sweet roll dough. Cover and let rise in a warm place until nearly double in size (30 to 45 minutes). Meanwhile, in a small mixing bowl combine cream cheese, egg yolk, sugar, flour, vanilla, and almond extract. Beat with an electric mixer on medium until well mixed and smooth. Preheat oven to 350°F. Spoon a rounded measuring teaspoon of the cream cheese mixture into the center of each coil.

3 Bake 15 to 18 minutes or until golden. Cool pastries slightly on a wire rack. Top the center of each pastry coil with ½ teaspoon jam. If desired, drizzle with Lemon Curd Icing. Serve warm or at room temperature.

PER SERVING 137 **CAL**; 4 g **FAT** (2 g **SAT**); 34 mg **CHOL**; 81 mg **SODIUM**; 22 g **CARB**; 1 g **FIBER**; 3 g **PRO**

LEMON CURD ICING: In a small bowl combine ¾ cup powdered sugar, 1 tablespoon lemon curd, ¼ teaspoon vanilla, and, if desired, ⅛ teaspoon almond extract. Stir in 1 tablespoon milk. If necessary, add additional milk, 1 teaspoon at a time, to reach drizzling consistency.

TURNOVERS: On a lightly floured surface roll one loaf of dough into a 12 x 9-inch rectangle. Cut twelve 3-inch squares from dough. Place a rounded measuring teaspoon of cream cheese mixture into the center of each square. Top each with ½ teaspoon jam. Fold each pastry square diagonally in half. Using the tines of a fork, seal edges. With fork, poke a few holes in the top of each triangle. Place on a baking sheet lined with parchment paper. Cover and let rise in a warm place until nearly double in size (30 to 45 minutes). Repeat with the remaining loaf of sweet roll dough, remaining cream cheese mixture, and remaining jam. Bake as directed in Step 3. If desired, drizzle with Lemon Curd Icing. Serve warm or at room temperature. Makes 24 servings.

ENVELOPES: On a lightly floured surface roll 1 loaf of dough into a 12 x 9-inch rectangle. Cut twelve 3-inch squares form dough. Place on a baking sheet lined with parchment paper. Place a rounded measuring teaspoon of cream cheese mixture into the center of each square. Top each with ½ teaspoon jam. Fold points to the center, forming an envelope. Pinch points together in the center to seal. (If necessary, lightly moisten points with water to seal.) Cover and let rise in a warm place until nearly double in size (30 to 45 minutes). Repeat with the remaining loaf of sweet roll dough, remaining cream cheese mixture, and remaining jam. Bake as directed in Step 3. If desired, drizzle with Lemon Curd Icing. Serve warm or at room temperature. Makes 24 servings.

Cinnamon Scones with Fruit Ribbons

Although few folks enjoy the texture of old-fashion holiday fruitcake, the thin layer of flavorful dried fruit in the middle of these tender scones will win rave reviews.

MAKES 12 servings   **PREP** 40 minutes   **STAND** 30 minutes   **BAKE** 35 minutes at 375°F   **COOL** 10 minutes

- ½ **cup chopped dried cranberries**
- ¼ **cup dried currants**
- 2 **tablespoons chopped candied orange peel**
- ¼ **cup brandy or orange juice**
- 3 **tablespoons butter, softened**
- ½ **cup packed dark brown sugar**
- 1 **tablespoon ground cinnamon**
- 1 **tablespoon all-purpose flour**
- 1 **cup quick-cooking oats**
- 2 **cups all-purpose flour**
- ⅓ **cup granulated sugar**
- ½ **teaspoon salt**
- ½ **cup butter, cut up**
- 2 **eggs**
- ⅓ **cup sour cream**
- ¼ **cup milk**
- 1 **teaspoon vanilla**
- 1 **egg white**
- 1 **tablespoon water**
- 1 **recipe Cinnamon-Sugar**

1 In a small saucepan combine cranberries, currants, orange peel, and brandy. Bring just to boiling over medium-high heat. Remove from heat, cover saucepan, and let stand for 30 minutes.

2 Drain and discard excess brandy from fruit mixture; set fruit aside. In a small bowl combine the 3 tablespoons butter, brown sugar, cinnamon, and the 1 tablespoon flour; mix well. Add reserved fruit; toss to combine. Set aside.

3 Preheat oven to 375°F. Lightly grease a 9 x 1½-inch round baking pan; set aside.

4 In a large bowl stir together oats, the 2 cups flour, the granulated sugar, and salt. Using a pastry blender, cut the ½ cup butter into flour mixture until mixture is the texture of cornmeal. Make a well in the center.

5 In a small bowl whisk together eggs, sour cream, milk, and vanilla. Add sour cream mixture all at once to flour mixture. Using a fork, stir just until moistened. Turn dough out onto a lightly floured surface. Knead dough by folding and gently pressing it for 3 to 4 turns. Divide dough in half.

6 Pat one half of dough evenly in prepared pan. Spread fruit mixture evenly over dough. On a lightly floured sheet of waxed paper pat second half dough into a 9-inch circle. Cut into 12 wedges. Using waxed paper, carefully invert cut circle on top of fruit mixture; remove waxed paper. Press gently on edges to seal layers together. In a small bowl whisk together egg white and water; brush on dough. Sprinkle with Cinnamon-Sugar.

7 Bake for 35 to 40 minutes or until golden brown. Cool in pan on wire rack for 10 minutes. Invert scones onto a large plate, then invert scones again onto a serving plate.

Cinnamon-Sugar: In a bowl stir together 2 teaspoons granulated sugar and ¼ teaspoon ground cinnamon.

PER SERVING 326 CAL; 13 g FAT (8 g SAT); 66 mg CHOL; 198 mg SODIUM; 45 g CARB; 2 g FIBER; 5 g PRO

Ooey-Gooey Monkey Bread

Sticky caramel goodness does not get any easier than this thanks to the use of refrigerated buttermilk biscuits. Consider making these on Saturday morning, when the kids can pitch in with the preparation.

MAKES 10 servings **PREP** 20 minutes **BAKE** 30 minutes at 350°F **STAND** 10 minutes

1 cup sugar
2 teaspoons ground cinnamon
½ cup butter, melted
2 12-ounce cans refrigerated buttermilk biscuits (20 biscuits total)
⅓ cup caramel-flavor ice cream topping
2 tablespoons maple syrup

1 Preheat oven to 350°F. Generously grease a 10-inch fluted tube pan or tube pan; set aside.

2 In a medium bowl stir together sugar and cinnamon; set aside. Place melted butter in another medium bowl. Using kitchen scissors, cut each biscuit into fourths. Toss biscuit pieces, several at a time, in melted butter, then in cinnamon-sugar to coat. Layer biscuit pieces in the prepared tube pan; press lightly. Sprinkle with any remaining cinnamon-sugar and drizzle with any remaining melted butter.

3 In a small bowl combine caramel topping and maple syrup. Drizzle mixture over biscuits.

4 Bake about 30 minutes or until golden and a wooden toothpick inserted near the center comes out clean. Let stand in pan for 10 minutes. Invert onto a large serving platter. Serve warm.

PER SERVING 298 **CAL**; 11 g **FAT** (6 g **SAT**); 25 mg **CHOL**; 500 mg **SODIUM**; 50 g **CARB**; 1 g **FIBER**; 3 g **PRO**

Caramel Rolls

Indianola, Iowa, resident Lana Ross, a long-time cooking and baking competitor at the Iowa State Fair, has become such an avid competitor that in 2012, she entered 81—that's right, 81—creations in various categories. Lana, who was raised on a farm, learned to make everything from scratch. She takes 2 weeks' vacation every year to work on her fair entries. She credits mashed potatoes and farm-fresh eggs as the ingredients that made her rolls a sweet success in the Tone's-sponsored cinnamon roll contest. Lana took overall honors in the cinnamon roll categories, including cinnamon, caramel, and non-traditions, which garnered her $3500.

MAKES 18 servings **PREP** 45 minutes **RISE** 1 hour 45 minutes **COOK** 15 minutes **BAKE** 20 minutes at 350°F

¼ **cup warm milk (100°F to 110°F)**

1 **envelope Fleischmann's active dry yeast (2¼ teaspoons)**

⅓ **cup butter or margarine, cut into slices**

¾ **cup milk**

½ **cup granulated sugar**

1½ **teaspoons salt**

½ **teaspoon Tone's 100% pure vanilla extract**

3 **eggs**

1 **cup mashed cooked potatoes (unseasoned)**

5 **to 5¾ cups all-purpose flour**

½ **cup butter or margarine**

1½ **cups packed brown sugar**

¼ **cup Karo light or dark corn syrup**

1 **teaspoon Tone's ground cinnamon**

½ **cup chopped pecans, toasted (see note, page 9)**

⅓ **cup butter, softened**

¾ **cup packed brown sugar**

2 **tablespoons Tone's ground cinnamon**

1 Pour the ¼ cup warm milk and yeast into a small bowl; let rest 5 minutes to soften yeast. Heat butter and ¾ cup milk until warm (100°F to 110°F); butter does need to completely melt.

2 Pour warm milk and butter mixture into large mixing bowl with the granulated sugar, 1½ teaspoons salt, and the vanilla. Add eggs, mashed potatoes, 2 cups of the flour ,and yeast mixture. Beat on medium for 3 minutes. Gradually add enough flour to make a soft dough. Turn out onto a lightly floured surface. Knead in enough of the remaining flour to make a moderately soft dough that is smooth and elastic (3 to 5 minutes). Place in a greased bowl, turning once to coat. Cover and let rise in a warm, draft-free place about 1 hour, until doubled in size.

3 For the caramel syrup, in a heavy saucepan combine ½ cup butter, the 1½ cups brown sugar, corn syrup, and cinnamon over low heat. Cook about 15 minutes or until syrup just starts to bubble around the edges of the pan. Remove from heat. Equally divide hot syrup between two greased 9-inch square pans. Sprinkle toasted pecans over syrup; gently stir to coat pecans. Set pans aside.

4 Punch dough down and divide in half. Roll out half of the dough onto a lightly floured surface to a 12 x 10-inch rectangle. Spread each with half of the softened butter. Combine ¾ cup brown sugar and cinnamon; sprinkle half the sugar-cinnamon evenly on dough. Roll up jelly-roll-style, starting from a long side. Slice into 9 rolls, placing cut sides down in pan on caramel syrup. Repeat with remaining dough. Cover and let rolls rise in warm, draft-free place until doubled in size, about 45 minutes.

5 Preheat oven to 350°F. Bake for 20 to 25 minutes or until golden. Remove from oven and let stand 2 minutes. Invert rolls onto serving platter or parchment paper. Serve warm.

PER SERVING 424 **CAL**; 16 g **FAT** (8 g **SAT**); 64 mg **CHOL**; 329 mg **SODIUM**; 67 g **CARB**; 2 g **FIBER**; 6 g **PRO**

Sunny Morning Biscuits

Upon his retirement from the insurance industry, Tennessee resident James Hayes rerouted his energies into volunteer work. Soon, he found that one of his longtime hobbies—baking—came in pretty handy. So when James—who delivered baked goods to ailing church friends, brought goodies to church suppers, and even prepared 200 biscuits a month for the church food pantry—caught wind of the International Biscuit Festival, he decided to give it a go. Inspired by a date and coconut scone he sampled in a South Carolina bakery, he devised a biscuit recipe featuring the same flavors, added a sunny orange glaze to their tops, and won First Prize in the Sweets category.

MAKES 10 servings **PREP** 20 minutes **BAKE** 12 minutes at 400°F

2	**cups self-rising flour**
⅓	**cup granulated sugar**
⅓	**cup butter**
½	**cup evaporated milk**
1	**egg, lightly beaten**
1	**teaspoon vanilla**
½	**cup chopped pitted dates**
½	**cup shredded coconut**
½	**powdered sugar**
3	**tablespoons orange juice**

1 Preheat oven to 400°F. Line a baking sheet with parchment paper; set aside. In a large bowl combine flour and granulated sugar. Using a pastry blender, cut in butter until mixture resembles coarse crumbs. In a small bowl combine milk, egg, and vanilla. Add to flour mixture, stirring with a folk just until combined. If too wet to handle, add more flour, a little at a time.

2 Turn dough out onto a lightly floured surface. Knead dough 8 to 10 times by folding and gently pressing it just until dough holds together. With a rolling pin, roll the dough to a 10 x 7-inch rectangle about ½ inch thick. Place the dates and coconut on the dough. Roll up, starting from a long side; pinch dough to seal seams. Use plain dental floss or 100%-cotton kitchen string to cut into 10 slices. Place about 2 inches apart on prepared baking sheet.

3 Bake 12 to 15 minutes or until golden brown. Cool biscuits on baking sheet on a wire rack.

4 In a small bowl combine powdered sugar and orange juice. Using a pastry brush, coat the tops of the hot biscuits.

PER SERVING 261 **CAL**; 9 g **FAT** (6 g **SAT**); 38 mg **CHOL**; 402 mg **SODIUM**; 42 g **CARB**; 2 g **FIBER**; 4 g **PRO**;

Chocolate Lover's Granola

A batch of this chocolate granola—studded with semisweet and white chocolate baking pieces—makes it impossible to get up on the wrong side of the bed. Small bags make perfect lunch box snacks as well.

MAKES 14 servings **PREP** 20 minutes
BAKE 30 minutes at 300°F

- 2 **cups regular rolled oats**
- 1 **cup sliced or slivered almonds, coarsely chopped, or chopped walnuts**
- ½ **cup flaked coconut (optional)**
- ½ **cup dry-roasted sunflower kernels**
- ¼ **cup toasted wheat germ**
- ¼ **cup flaxseed meal**
- ½ **cup honey**
- 2 **tablespoons vegetable oil**
- 2 **ounces bittersweet chocolate**
- 1 **cup white chocolate baking pieces**
- 1 **cup semisweet chocolate pieces**

1 Preheat oven to 300°F. Grease a 15 x 10 x 1-inch baking pan; set aside. In a large bowl combine oats, nuts, coconut (if desired), sunflower kernels, wheat germ, and flaxseed meal. In a small saucepan combine the honey, oil, and chocolate; heat over low heat until chocolate is melted. Stir into oat mixture. Spread evenly into prepared pan.

2 Bake for 30 to 35 minutes or until light brown, stirring after 20 minutes. Spread on a large piece of foil; cool completely. Before serving, stir in 1 cup white chocolate baking pieces and 1 cup semisweet chocolate pieces.

PER SERVING: 370 **CAL**, 20 g **FAT** (8 g **SAT**), 0 mg **CHOL**; 26 mg **SODIUM**; 44 g **CARB**, 5 g **FIBER**; 6 g **PRO**

Cranberry-Pistachio Granola: Prepare Classic Granola as directed, except substitute 1½ cups shelled pistachio nuts for the 1 cup almonds or walnuts. Before serving, stir in 1½ cups dried cranberries.

PER SERVING: 269 **CAL**; 13 g **FAT** (1 g **SAT**); 0 mg **CHOL**; 3 mg **SODIUM**; 36 g **CARB**, 5 g **FIBER**; 7 g **PRO**

Berry Smoothie

What a gold mine of nutritious morning meals! This recipe—with 6 variations—provides one week's worth of quick and easy drinkable breakfasts.

MAKES 2 servings **START TO FINISH** 10 minutes

- 1 **6-ounce carton plain yogurt**
- ½ **cup orange juice or orange juice blend**
- 2 **tablespoons honey or sugar**
- ¼ **teaspoon vanilla**
- 1 **cup small ice cubes or crushed ice**
- ½ **cup halved fresh strawberries or fresh raspberries**

1 In a blender combine yogurt, orange juice, honey, vanilla, ice cubes, and strawberries. Cover and blend until nearly smooth.

PER SERVING 147 **CAL**; 1 g **FAT** (1 g **SAT**); 5 mg **CHOL**; 61 mg **SODIUM**; 30 g **CARB**, 0 g **FIBER**; 5 g **PRO**

Banana-Blueberry Smoothie: Prepare as above, except substitute blueberry yogurt for the plain yogurt and use half a ripe banana and ½ cup fresh or frozen blueberries instead of the strawberries or raspberries.

Banana-Chocolate Smoothie: Prepare as above, except substitute vanilla yogurt for the plain yogurt, milk for the orange juice, chocolate-flavored syrup for the honey and use half a ripe banana instead of the strawberries or raspberries.

Mango Smoothie: Prepare as above, except use ½ cup chopped fresh or frozen mango instead of the strawberries or raspberries.

Mocha Smoothie: Prepare as above, except substitute coffee-flavored yogurt for the plain yogurt, milk for the orange juice, and chocolate-flavored syrup for the honey and omit the strawberries or raspberries.

Orange Dream: Prepare as above, except substitute orange yogurt for the plain yogurt and use ½ cup mandarin orange sections instead of the strawberries or raspberries.

Peanut Butter-Banana Smoothie: Prepare as above, except substitute vanilla yogurt for the plain yogurt, milk for the orange juice, and use half a ripe banana and 2 tablespoons creamy peanut butter instead of the strawberries or raspberries.

BERRY SMOOTHIE

meals in minutes

Quick and easy home-cooked meals from kitchen to table in 30 minutes or less.

SUNDAY DINNER STEW

BEEF

Cowboy Steak Tacos, 61

Italian Fried Steak with Roasted
Pepper Pesto, 59

Sunday Dinner Stew, 57

CHICKEN

Blue Cheese-and-Olives-Stuffed
Chicken, 63

Chicken and Vegetable Spaghetti, 64

Chicken Piccata, 65

The Original Chicken à la King, 61

PORK

Apple-Glazed Pork Loaves, 55

Bacon and Blue Cheese Dinner Pies, 59

Bacon-Wrapped Pork and Beans, 54

Five-Spice Pork Kabobs, 53

Mustard-Glazed Pork Chops, 52

Pea Soup with Ham, 56

FISH AND SEAFOOD

Catfish with Succotash Salad, 67

Lemon Shrimp and Pasta, 69

Shrimp with Peppers and Corn, 68

Spice-Rubbed Salmon, 67

MEATLESS

Autumn Couscous Bowl, 73

Browned Butter and Garlic Pasta, 70

Fettuccine Alfredo, 73

Mustard-Glazed Pork Chops

Great cooks know that combining tangy mustard and sweet apricot preserves is one of the quickest and easiest tricks to take pork or chicken from simple to simply sensational. Try it—you'll agree.

MAKES 4 servings   **START TO FINISH** 25 minutes

4	**½-inch-thick bone-in pork chops**
	Salt and black pepper
2	**teaspoons olive oil**
1	**large onion, cut into thin wedges**
½	**cup apricot preserves**
1	**tablespoon Dijon or spicy mustard**
¼	**cup water**
1	**teaspoon paprika**
½	**teaspoon ground nutmeg**
	Fresh sage leaves (optional)

1 Season pork with salt and pepper. In a large skillet heat olive oil over medium-high heat. Add pork and onion to skillet. Cook 3 minutes; turn pork and onion. Cook 3 minutes more.

2 Meanwhile, in a small microwave-safe bowl combine preserves, mustard, ¼ cup water, paprika, and nutmeg. Heat in microwave for 1 to 2 minutes or until melted. Pour over pork in skillet. Reduce heat to medium. Cook, covered, 8 minutes or until chops are 145°F. Let chops stand for 3 minutes.

3 Divide pork and onion among four serving plates; top with sage.

PER SERVING 503 **CAL**; 32 g **FAT** (11 g **SAT**); 89 mg **CHOL**; 313 mg **SODIUM**; 31 g **CARB**; 1 g **FIBER**; 20 g **PRO**

Five-Spice Pork Kabobs

If you have trouble finding Chinese five-spice powder, just make your own. To do so, combine 1½ tablespoons ground cinnamon, 1 teaspoon anise seeds, ¾ teaspoon fennel seeds, ¾ teaspoon coarsely black pepper, and ¼ teaspoon ground cloves in a small jar. Shake well and store, tightly sealed, in a cool place.

MAKES 4 servings **PREP** 20 minutes **GRILL** 4 minutes

2 **tablespoons ketchup**
1 **tablespoon soy sauce**
2 **teaspoons packed brown sugar**
1 **teaspoon Chinese five-spice powder**
1½ **pounds pork tenderloin**
8 **bamboo or metal skewers***
¼ **cup peanuts**
¼ **cup cilantro sprigs**
   Cooked pasta (optional)

1 For sauce, in a small bowl combine ketchup, soy sauce, brown sugar, and five-spice powder. For kabobs, trim tenderloin, slice thinly, then thread slices onto skewers. Brush skewered meat with some of the sauce.

2 For a charcoal grill, grill kabobs directly over medium-hot coals for 2 to 3 minutes. Brush with remaining sauce. Turn kabobs; grill 2 to 3 minutes more or until no longer pink and juices run clear (145°F). Serve in bowls on a bed of cooked pasta, if desired. Sprinkle with peanuts and cilantro.

***Note:** Soak bamboo skewers in water 30 minutes before using to prevent the skewers from burning.

PER SERVING 280 **CAL**; 11 g **FAT** (3 g **SAT**); 111 mg **CHOL**; 458 mg **SODIUM**; 7 g **CARB**; 1 g **FIBER**; 38 g **PRO**

Bacon-Wrapped Pork and Beans

Thin medallions of lean pork tenderloin remain moist and succulent when bacon-wrapped and grilled. Serve the pork with this yummy, five-ingredient pinto bean mixture and you'll have a full meal prepared in just half an hour.

MAKES 4 servings **START TO FINISH** 30 minutes

1	1½- to 1¾-inch-thick center-cut pork tenderloin
	Salt
	Black pepper
8	slices bacon
16	green onions
1	15-ounce can pinto beans, rinsed and drained
1	cup cherry or grape tomatoes, halved
⅓	cup ketchup
2	tablespoons water
1	teaspoon yellow mustard

1 Trim fat from meat. Cut meat crosswise into eight pieces. Sprinkle lightly with salt and pepper. Wrap 1 slice of bacon around each meat slice; secure with a small skewer or wooden pick.

2 For a charcoal grill, arrange medium-hot coals around a drip pan. Test for medium heat above pan. Place meat on grill rack over drip pan. Cover and grill about 15 minutes or until meat is slightly pink in center and juices run clear (145°F), turning once halfway through grilling. (For a gas grill, preheat grill. Reduce heat to medium. Adjust for indirect cooking. Cover and grill as above.)

3 While meat is grilling, chop 4 of the green onions; set aside. Add the remaining green onions to grill directly over heat. Cover and grill for 3 to 4 minutes or just until tender, turning occasionally.

4 Meanwhile, in a medium saucepan combine chopped green onions, beans, tomatoes, ketchup, the water, and mustard. Bring to boiling; reduce heat. Simmer, covered, until heated through. Keep warm. Serve grilled pork with green onions and beans.

PER SERVING 452 **CAL**; 11 g **FAT** (4 g **SAT**); 107 mg **CHOL**; 1,147 mg **SODIUM**; 33 g **CARB**; 8 g **FIBER**; 55 g **PRO**

Apple-Glazed Pork Loaves

If you're unable to find ciabatta buns on your bakery shelves, slice a full loaf of ciabatta into medium-thick chunks or use a loaf of French bread to do the same.

MAKES 4 servings **PREP** 20 minutes **BAKE** 12 minutes at 425°F

½ cup apple jelly

1 tablespoon Dijon mustard

2 medium apples

2 eggs, lightly beaten

½ teaspoon salt

½ teaspoon black pepper

1 pound ground pork

1 medium sweet potato, chopped

⅛ teaspoon cayenne pepper (optional)

1 tablespoon olive oil

2 ciabatta buns, split and toasted

1 Preheat oven to 425°F. Grease a 15 x 10 x 1-inch baking pan; set aside. For glaze, place jelly in a small microwave-safe bowl. Heat on high about 20 seconds or until melted. Stir in mustard; set aside.

2 Core and chop 1 of the apples. In a large bowl combine half of the chopped apple, the eggs, salt, and black pepper. Add ground pork; mix well. Shape meat mixture into four 6 x 2-inch loaves. Place in the prepared baking pan. Spoon some of the glaze over loaves. Bake, uncovered, for 8 minutes. Thinly slice the remaining apple. Top loaves with apple slices; drizzle with the remaining glaze. Bake, uncovered, about 4 minutes more or until done (145°F).

3 Meanwhile, in another small microwave-safe bowl cook sweet potato on high about 4 minutes or until nearly tender. In a medium skillet cook the remaining chopped apple, sweet potato, and, if desired, cayenne pepper in hot oil over medium-high heat about 3 minutes or until tender, stirring occasionally. To serve, place pork loaves on ciabatta bun halves. Top with sweet potato mixture.

PER SERVING 697 **CAL**; 32 g **FAT** (11 g **SAT**); 187 mg **CHOL**; 842 mg **SODIUM**; 74 g **CARB**; 5 g **FIBER**; 28 g **PRO**

Pea Soup with Ham

Here, canned split pea soup is doctored up with a handful of flavorful additions that take the winter-classic soup from a two-hour endeavor into a quick and easy 25-minute sprint.

MAKES 4 servings **START TO FINISH** 25 minutes

- 2   leeks, white parts sliced
- 2   teaspoons olive oil
- 2   19-ounce cans ready-to-serve green split pea with bacon soup
- 1½ cups apple juice
- 2   carrots, peeled and chopped
- ½   cup diced cooked ham
- ½   teaspoon black pepper

1 In a large saucepan cook leeks in hot oil over medium heat for 3 minutes or just until tender. Remove a few leeks with a slotted spoon and set aside. Stir in soup, apple juice, carrots, ham, and pepper. Bring to boiling. Reduce heat and simmer, covered, 15 minutes or until carrots are tender.

2 Ladle into serving bowls and top with reserved leeks .

PER SERVING 291 **CAL**; 4 g **FAT** (1 g **SAT**); 3 mg **CHOL**; 1,038 mg **SODIUM**; 51 g **CARB**; 7 g **FIBER**; 11 g **PRO**

Sunday Dinner Stew

Savory, satisfying beef stew, a dish that usually takes a few hours to reach perfection, does so here in a mere 25 minutes thanks to refrigerated cooked beef tips.

MAKES 4 servings **START TO FINISH** 25 minutes

- 1   pound small new potatoes
- 3   large carrots, halved lengthwise and cut up
- 1   17-ounce package refrigerated cooked beef tips with gravy
- 1¼ cups water
-     Fresh or dried thyme

1 Rinse potatoes. Halve or quarter large potatoes for fairly uniform size. Place potatoes in a large microwave-safe bowl. Cover with vented plastic wrap and cook on high for 5 minutes. Add carrots; cover and cook for 5 to 7 minutes, just until potatoes and carrots are tender.

2 In a Dutch oven combine potatoes and carrots, beef tips in gravy, and the water. Cook over medium-high heat just until bubbly around edges. Cover and cook for 5 minutes more or until heated through. Ladle into bowls. Sprinkle with thyme.

PER SERVING 302 **CAL**; 9 g **FAT** (3 g **SAT**); 52 mg **CHOL**; 686 mg **SODIUM**; 36 g **CARB**; 6 g **FIBER**; 22 g **PRO**

SUNDAY DINNER STEW

ITALIAN FRIED STEAK WITH
ROASTED PEPPER PESTO

Italian Fried Steak with Roasted Pepper Pesto

Quick-cooking cube steaks go from ho-hum to heavenly when breaded in a mixture of crumbs and Parmesan cheese and sauced with a luscious, two-ingredient pesto preparation.

MAKES 4 servings **START TO FINISH** 30 minutes

- ½   **cup seasoned fine dry bread crumbs**
- ½   **cup grated Romano or Parmesan cheese**
- 1   **egg**
- 2   **tablespoons water**
- 1½ **pounds beef cube steak**
     Olive oil
- 1   **12-ounce jar roasted red sweet peppers, drained**
- ⅔   **cup thinly sliced fresh basil leaves**

1 In a shallow dish combine crumbs and half the cheese. In another shallow dish beat together egg and water. Cut meat into 8 equal-size portions; lightly sprinkle with salt and pepper. Dip in egg mixture, then crumb mixture; press lightly to coat.

2 In a large skillet heat 1 tablespoon olive oil over medium-high heat. Working in two batches, cook steak about 5 minutes per side, adding more oil as needed. Remove to a serving platter; cover to keep warm. Carefully wipe skillet clean.

3 Meanwhile, for sauce, in a blender or food processor combine drained peppers and remaining cheese. Process until nearly smooth. Finely chop ½ cup of the basil; set aside. Transfer sauce to hot skillet and heat through. Remove from heat. Stir in finely chopped basil. Pour sauce over steaks. Sprinkle with remaining basil.

PER SERVING 425 **CAL**; 21 g **FAT** (8 g **SAT**); 130 mg **CHOL**; 645 mg **SODIUM**; 15 g **CARB**; 2 g **FIBER**; 43 g **PRO**

Bacon and Blue Cheese Dinner Pies

Corn muffin mix forms the crust for these savory bacon, apple, and cheese tarts. Don't limit this recipe to dinnertime only—the pies make a beautiful brunch dish as well.

MAKES 4 servings **PREP** 15 minutes
BAKE 15 minutes at 400°F

- 4   **slices bacon**
- 1   **8.5-ounce package corn muffin mix**
- ½   **cup all-purpose flour**
- 1   **teaspoon chili powder**
- 1   **egg, lightly beaten**
- ¼   **cup milk**
- ⅓   **cup blue cheese crumbles**
- 1   **large Golden Delicious apple, cored and thinly sliced**
     Fresh thyme (optional)

1 Preheat oven to 400°F. Grease two baking sheets or line with parchment paper; set aside. In a skillet cook bacon until crisp. Drain; reserve 2 tablespoons drippings. Chop bacon.

2 Meanwhile, in a medium bowl combine muffin mix, flour, chili powder, egg, and milk with a fork. Use your hands to knead dough until it comes together. Divide dough into four portions. Place two portions on each prepared baking sheet and press to 6-inch circles using floured hands.

3 Top circles with half of the cheese and a layer of apple slices, leaving a 1-inch border. Fold edges around apple slices, using floured hands if necessary. Brush apples and crust with 1 to 2 tablespoons reserved bacon drippings.

4 Place baking sheets on separate oven racks. Bake for 10 minutes. Top each pie with remaining blue cheese and the bacon; return to separate racks and bake for 5 to 7 minutes more until edges are golden. If desired, sprinkle with thyme.

PER SERVING 524 **CAL**; 19 g **FAT** (6 g **SAT**); 79 mg **CHOL**; 890 mg **SODIUM**; 72 g **CARB**; 3 g **FIBER**; 15 g **PRO**

COWBOY STEAK TACOS

Cowboy Steak Tacos

In the days when nothing was wasted, leftover coffee was found to be an amazing flavor enhancer, especially when used in beef dishes. Just use the cold coffee left in your morning pot to make tacos that will bring out your inner cowboy—or cowgirl.

MAKES 4 servings **START TO FINISH** 30 minutes

- 1 **pound beef breakfast steaks (thinly sliced eye of round)**
- ¼ **teaspoon salt**
- 1 **cup strong coffee**
- 2 **tablespoons ketchup**
- 2 **teaspoons chili powder**
- 2 **teaspoons vegetable oil**
- 1 **small red onion, thinly sliced**
- 1 **red or green sweet pepper, thinly sliced**
- 12 **6-inch tortillas (corn, flour, or whole wheat)**
- ¾ **cup prepared corn relish**
   Fresh cilantro leaves (optional)

1 Thinly slice the steaks (as for stir-fry). Sprinkle steaks with salt; set aside. For sauce, in a small bowl whisk together coffee, ketchup, and chili powder.

2 In a large skillet heat oil over medium-high heat; add beef. Cook and stir for 2 to 3 minutes or until browned on all sides. Add sauce, onion, and sweet pepper. Cook for 6 to 8 minutes or until vegetables are tender and sauce is thickened.

3 Meanwhile, wrap tortillas in paper towels. Warm in the microwave on high for 30 seconds. Spoon steak and vegetable mixture on tortillas. Top with corn relish and, if desired, sprinkle with cilantro.

PER SERVING 596 **CAL**; 20 g **FAT** (6 g **SAT**); 74 mg **CHOL**; 1,169 mg **SODIUM**; 71 g **CARB**; 4 g **FIBER**; 32 g **PRO**

The Original Chicken à la King

The name of this utterly rich dish is a pretty good clue that it is truly fit for a king.

MAKES 4 servings **START TO FINISH** 25 minutes

- 2 **tablespoons butter**
- ½ **cup thinly sliced mushrooms**
- 2 **tablespoons finely chopped green sweet pepper**
- 1 **tablespoon all-purpose flour**
- ¼ **teaspoon salt**
- 1 **cup half-and-half or light cream**
- 2 **tablespoons butter, softened**
- 1 **egg yolk**
- 1½ **teaspoons lemon juice**
- ½ **teaspoon onion juice (optional)**
- ¼ **teaspoon paprika**
- 1½ **cups chopped cooked chicken**
- 1 **tablespoon diced pimiento, drained**
- 1 **teaspoon sherry**
- 4 **baked pastry shells**

1 In a large skillet melt 2 tablespoons butter over medium heat. Add mushrooms and sweet pepper; cook until tender. Stir in the flour and salt. Add half-and-half all at once; cook and stir until thickened and bubbly.

2 In a medium bowl stir together the 2 tablespoons softened butter and egg yolks. Add the lemon juice, onion juice (if desired), and paprika. Stir about 1 cup of the half-and-half mixture into the egg mixture; add to the half-and-half mixture in the skillet. Cook and stir over medium heat until bubbly. Stir in chicken, pimiento, and sherry; heat through. Serve over baked pastry shells.

PER SERVING 297 **CAL**; 19 g total **FAT** (10 g **SAT**); 163 mg **CHOL**; 346 mg **SODIUM**; 12 g **CARB**; 1 g **FIBER**; 20 g **PRO**

Blue Cheese-and-Olive-Stuffed Chicken

According to judges, the stuffed chicken recipe that California cook and food blogger Jennifer Richmond of kitchycooking.com submitted to Lindsay's Love This Recipe Contest delivered everything they were looking for. Described as "truly bursting with style, flavor, originality, and the embodiment of the challenge of the contest," Julie's recipe—which came to her as a result of wondering how blue cheese-stuffed olives could be used other than in cocktails—took Grand Prize, enabling the mom of two to walk away with a $1,000 prize.

MAKES 4 servings **PREP** 30 minutes **BAKE** 15 minutes at 400°F

4   **cloves garlic, peeled**
1   **cup Lindsay Naturals Green Ripe California Pitted Olives or Lindsay Pitted Olives**
2   **tablespoons crumbled blue cheese**
2   **tablespoons olive oil**
4   **5- to 6-ounce skinless, boneless chicken breast halves**
1   **teaspoon kosher salt**
½   **teaspoon freshly ground black pepper**
1   **egg, lightly beaten**
¾   **cup panko (Japanese-style bread crumbs)**

1 Preheat oven to 400°F. With food processor running, drop garlic through the feed tube of a food processor until minced. Add olives, blue cheese, and 1 tablespoon of the olive oil; cover and pulse until olives are finely chopped.

2 Using a sharp knife, cut a pocket in each breast half by cutting horizontally through the thickest portion to, but not through, the opposite side. Spoon about ¼ cup olive stuffing into each pocket. Gently press edges together to seal pockets. Sprinkle with salt and pepper.

3 Place beaten egg in a shallow dish. Place panko in second shallow dish. Dip stuffed chicken in egg to moisten and in panko to coat.

4 In a large nonstick oven-safe skillet heat remaining 1 tablespoon oil over medium heat. Add chicken. Cook for 2 minutes or until golden brown. Carefully turn chicken and place skillet in oven. Bake about 15 minutes or until chicken is no longer pink (170°F) and golden brown.

PER SERVING 350 **CAL**; 19 g **FAT** (19 g **SAT**); 140 mg **CHOL**; 1,339 mg **SODIUM**; 10 g **CARB**; 2 g **FIBER** ; 34 g **PRO**

Chicken and Vegetable Spaghetti

Italians often reserve part of their pasta-cooking water as a slurry to use in sauce. Doing so allows the starch—released by the cooking pasta—to help thicken and give body to the sauce.

MAKES 4 servings   **START TO FINISH** 35 minutes

- 12 **ounces dried spaghetti**
- 1 **tablespoon olive oil**
- 8 **ounces skinless, boneless chicken breast halves, cut into bite-size pieces**
- 8 **ounces Broccolini, trimmed or broccoli, cut up**
- 2 **cups pearl onions, peeled* (8 ounces)**
- 1 **teaspoon dried parsley flakes (optional)**
- ½ **teaspoon salt (optional)**
  Crushed red pepper (optional)
- 1¼ **cups yellow or red cherry tomatoes (8 ounces)**
- 1 **cup chicken broth**

1 Cook spaghetti according to package direction. Reserve 1 cup pasta water; drain spaghetti.

2 Meanwhile, in a large skillet heat oil over medium-high heat. Add chicken; cook, stirring occasionally, until browned about 3 to 4 minutes. Add broccolini and onions. If desired, sprinkle with dried parsley, salt, and crushed red pepper. Cook, stirring frequently, for 5 minutes.

3 Add tomatoes, chicken broth, reserved pasta water, and cooked spaghetti. Simmer, uncovered, about 5 minutes or until the broth is slightly reduced and vegetables are tender

*Note: To easily peel pearl onions, add them to boiling water for 3 minutes before cooking pasta. Remove with a slotted spoon, cool slightly, then peel. Use the same water to cook pasta. As an alternative, use frozen pearl onions.

PER SERVING 453 **CAL**; 6 g **FAT** (1 g **SAT**); 34 mg **CHOL**; 318 mg **SODIUM**; 71 g **CARB**; 5 g **FIBER**; 27 g **PRO**

Chicken Piccata

If you do not have a meat mallet for pounding the chicken breasts, rely on your trusty rolling pin. It will do a great job!

MAKES 4 servings **START TO FINISH** 25 minutes

2 **8-ounce skinless, boneless chicken breasts, cut in half horizontally**
¼ **teaspoon salt**
¼ **teaspoon black pepper**
1 **tablespoon butter**
2 **cloves garlic, minced**
½ **cup reduced-sodium chicken broth**
1 **medium lemon, thinly sliced**
2 **tablespoons capers**

1 Place each chicken breast portion between two pieces of plastic wrap. Using the flat side of a meat mallet, pound chicken lightly to about ¼-inch thickness. Remove plastic wrap. Sprinkle chicken with salt and pepper.

2 In a large skillet melt butter over medium-high heat. Add chicken; cook for 6 to 8 minutes or until browned and no longer pink in center, turning once halfway through cooking. Remove chicken from skillet; set aside.

3 For piccata topping, add garlic to the hot skillet; cook for 30 seconds to 1 minute or until lightly browned. Add chicken broth to skillet, scraping up any browned bits from skillet. Bring to boiling. Add lemon slices and capers. Cover; reduce heat to low. Cook for 4 to 5 minutes or until lemon slices are softened and releasing juices. Return chicken to skillet; heat through.

4 To serve, spoon topping over chicken.

PER SERVING 161 **CAL**; 4 g **FAT** (2 g **SAT**); 73 mg **CHOL**; 440 mg **SODIUM**; 4 g **CARB**; 2 g **FIBER**; 27 g **PRO**

SPICE-RUBBED SALMON

Spice-Rubbed Salmon

If you're worried about turning fish on the grill, don't be. Just make sure to grease the grill generously, use a wide metal spatula for turning, and do it like you mean business.

MAKES 4 servings **START TO FINISH** 20 minutes

- 2 **teaspoons chili powder**
- 1 **teaspoon ground cumin**
- 1 **teaspoon packed brown sugar**
- ¼ **teaspoon salt**
- ⅛ **teaspoon black pepper**
- 4 **5-ounce skinless salmon fillets**
- 1 **small cabbage, cut into 6 wedges**
- 2 **to 3 tablespoons cooking oil**
- 1 **large carrot**
  Orange wedges

1 In small bowl mix chili powder, cumin, brown sugar, salt, and pepper. Rub spice mixture on salmon. Brush cabbage wedges with 1 tablespoon of the oil.

2 On a charcoal grill place salmon and cabbage on the greased rack of an uncovered grill, directly over medium coals. Grill salmon 4 to 6 minutes for each half-inch of thickness or until it flakes when tested with a fork, turning once halfway through cooking time. Grill cabbage 6 to 8 minutes, turning once.

3 Meanwhile, peel carrot and cut into wide strips. Remove salmon and cabbage from grill. Coarsely cut cabbage; combine with carrot and 1 to 2 tablespoons remaining oil. Season with salt and pepper. Serve with oranges.

PER SERVING 380 **CAL**; 23 g **FAT** (4 g **SAT**); 84 mg **CHOL**; 284 mg **SODIUM**; 14 g **CARB**; 5 g **FIBER**; 31 g **PRO**

Catfish with Succotash Salad

U.S. farmed catfish—raised in ponds with circulating water and fed a vegetarian diet—is one of the most environmentally friendly sustainable seafood choices.

MAKES 4 servings **PREP** 20 minutes **GRILL** 6 minutes

- 4 **4- to 6-ounce fresh or frozen skinless catfish fillets, about ½ inch thick**
  Olive oil
  Garlic salt
  Black pepper
- 2 **cups frozen lima beans**
- 1 **cup corn relish**
- 1 **cup fresh baby spinach**

1 Thaw fish, if frozen. Rinse fish; pat dry with paper towels. Brush fish with olive oil and sprinkle with garlic salt and pepper; set aside.

2 Cook lima beans according to package directions. Place beans in a colander and cool quickly by running under cold water; drain. Set aside.

3 Place fish in a well-greased grill basket. For a charcoal grill, place grill basket on grill rack directly over medium coals. Grill for 6 to 9 minutes or until fish begins to flake easily when tested with a fork, turning basket once halfway through grilling. (For a gas grill, preheat grill. Reduce heat to medium. Place grill basket on grill rack directly over heat; cover and grill as above.)

4 To serve, place fish on serving platter. In a bowl toss together cooked lima beans, corn relish, and spinach. Serve with fish.

PER SERVING 372 **CAL**; 12 g **FAT** (3 g **SAT**); 53 mg **CHOL**; 509 mg **SODIUM**; 41 g **CARB**; 5 g **FIBER**; 24 g **PRO**

Shrimp with Peppers and Corn

There's no need to thaw the frozen shrimp for this Southwestern-flavor skillet supper—they'll cook quickly to perfection in the rich, vegetable-packed sauce.

MAKES 4 servings **START TO FINISH** 25 minutes

- **1   8.8-ounce pouch cooked long grain rice**
- **1   14.5-ounce can diced tomatoes with chili seasoning**
- **½   teaspoon salt**
- **½   teaspoon black pepper**
- **½   teaspoon ground cumin**
- **2   tablespoons olive oil or butter**
- **1   cup sliced baby or diced sweet peppers**
- **1   cup frozen whole kernel corn, thawed**
- **2   cloves garlic, minced**
- **1   pound peeled and deveined medium raw shrimp**
  Fresh parsley

1 In a small saucepan combine rice and undrained tomatoes. In a small bowl mix together salt, pepper, and the cumin; stir half into the rice. Cover and cook over medium heat until heated through. Reduce heat to low; cover and keep warm.

2 Meanwhile, in a 12-inch skillet heat oil over medium-high heat. Add peppers and corn. Cook, stirring occasionally, for 3 to 4 minutes. Stir in garlic. Sprinkle shrimp with remaining salt-cumin mixture. Add shrimp to skillet. Cook until shrimp are opaque and peppers are crisp tender (2 to 5 minutes, depending on size of shrimp).

3 Serve shrimp and peppers over rice; sprinkle with parsley.

PER SERVING 355 **CAL**; 11 g **FAT** (1 g **SAT**); 172 mg **CHOL**; 944 mg **SODIUM**; 38 g **CARB**; 4 g **FIBER**; 27 g **PRO**

Lemon Shrimp and Pasta

As baby spinach leaves wilt in the lemony-garlicky sauce, they not only add vivid green splashes of color to this simple supper but notch up the nutritional value as well.

MAKES 4 servings **START TO FINISH** 25 minutes

12 **ounces frozen peeled and deveined medium shrimp, thawed**
1 **lemon**
8 **ounces dried fettuccine**
2 **tablespoons olive oil**
3 **to 4 cloves garlic, thinly sliced**
6 **cups fresh baby spinach**
½ **teaspoon dried Italian seasoning, crushed**
   Salt
   Black pepper
   Fresh dill (optional)

1 Rinse shrimp; pat dry with paper towels. Finely shred 1 teaspoon peel from the lemon; set peel aside. Juice the lemon over a bowl; set juice aside. Cook pasta according to package directions.

2 Meanwhile, in large skillet heat olive oil over medium heat. Cook garlic in hot oil for 1 minute. Add shrimp; cook for 3 to 4 minutes or until shrimp are opaque, turning frequently. Add spinach and the drained pasta; toss just until spinach begins to wilt. Stir in Italian seasoning, the lemon peel, and 2 tablespoons of the lemon juice. Season to taste with salt and pepper. If desired, top with fresh dill.

PER SERVING 359 **CAL**; 9 g **FAT** (1 g **SAT**); 107 mg **CHOL**; 696 mg **SODIUM**; 50 g **CARB**; 5 g **FIBER**; 21 g **PRO**

Browned Butter and Garlic Pasta

Here's another way to toast nuts, and with this method, you can keep an eye on them! Simply place the nuts in a dry skillet and shake the skillet gently over medium heat until nuts are golden.

MAKES 12 servings **START TO FINISH** 30 minutes

1   pound dried penne, campanelle, or other shaped pasta
⅓   cup butter
3   cloves garlic, thinly sliced
¼   teaspoon cracked black pepper
⅓   cup slivered almonds, toasted (see note, page 9)
3   tablespoons olive oil
1   5-ounce package fresh spinach, large stems removed
½   cup oil-packed dried tomatoes, drained and snipped, or golden raisins
1   cup finely shredded Parmigiano-Reggiano or Parmesan cheese (4 ounces)
     Salt
     Cracked black pepper
     Shaved or finely shredded Parmigiano-Reggiano or Parmesan cheese (optional)

1 In a Dutch oven cook pasta according to package directions; drain. Return pasta to hot Dutch oven; cover and keep warm.

2 Meanwhile, in a large skillet melt butter over medium-low heat. Add garlic and the ¼ teaspoon pepper; cook just until garlic is golden and soft and butter is light brown, stirring frequently and watching carefully. Remove from heat. Stir in almonds and oil. Drizzle garlic butter over cooked pasta; toss gently to coat. Cover and keep warm.

3 In the same skillet (do not clean) cook spinach and dried tomatoes about 1 minute or just until spinach is wilted. Add spinach mixture and the 1 cup cheese to pasta; toss gently to combine. Season to taste with salt and additional pepper. Transfer to a serving platter or bowl. If desired, serve with additional cheese.

PER SERVING 271 **CAL**; 13 g **FAT** (5 g **SAT**); 18 mg **CHOL**; 222 mg **SODIUM**; 31 g **CARB**; 2 g **FIBER**; 9 g **PRO**

AUTUMN COUSCOUS BOWL

Autumn Couscous Bowl

To make it easier to peel tough-skinned butternut squash, pierce the squash in several places with a fork, then microwave on high for 1½ minutes.

MAKES 4 servings   **START TO FINISH** 30 minutes

- 1   **2-pound butternut squash, peeled and chopped into ½-inch pieces (about 4 cups)**
- 2   **cups small cauliflower florets**
- ½   **teaspoon each salt and black pepper**
      Nonstick cooking spray
- 1   **10-ounce package couscous**
- 3   **tablespoons butter**
- ¼   **cup sweet Asian chili sauce**
- ¼   **cup shelled pistachio nuts**
      Fresh thyme (optional)

1 Preheat broiler. Place squash and 2 tablespoons water in a large microwave-safe bowl; cover with vented plastic wrap. Cook on high for 5 to 8 minutes, until crisp tender, stirring once.

2 Transfer squash along with cauliflower to a 15 x 10 x 1-inch baking pan. Sprinkle with salt and pepper then lightly coat with cooking spray. Broil 4 to 5 inches from heat for 10 to 12 minutes, until tender and beginning to brown, stirring once halfway through broiling time.

3 Meanwhile, prepare couscous according to package directions; set aside. In a small microwave-safe bowl combine the butter and chili sauce. Cook on high just until butter is melted.

4 Divide couscous among 4 shallow bowls. Top with vegetables, pistachios, chili-butter, and thyme.

PER SERVING 521 **CAL**; 13 g **FAT** (6 g **SAT**); 23 mg **CHOL**; 633 mg **SODIUM**; 90 g **CARB**; 9 g **FIBER**; 14 g **PRO**

Fettuccine Alfredo

Is there anyone that doesn't adore this richer-than-rich Italian classic? By using the recipe's two easy variations, you can serve it even more!

MAKES 4 servings   **START TO FINISH** 30 minutes

- 8   **ounces dried fettuccine**
- 2   **cloves garlic, minced**
- 2   **tablespoons butter or margarine**
- 1   **cup whipping cream**
- ½   **teaspoon salt**
- ⅛   **teaspoon black pepper**
- ½   **cup grated Parmesan cheese**
      Grated or finely shredded Parmesan cheese (optional)

1 In a large saucepan cook fettuccine according to package directions; drain.

2 Meanwhile, in a large saucepan cook garlic in hot butter over medium-high heat for 1 minute. Add cream, salt, and pepper. Bring to boiling; reduce heat. Boil gently, uncovered, for 3 minutes or until mixture begins to thicken. Remove from heat and stir in ½ cup Parmesan cheese. Drain pasta. Add pasta to hot sauce. Toss to combine. If desired, sprinkle each serving with additional cheese.

PER SERVING 514 **CAL**; 32 g **FAT** (19 g **SAT**); 107 mg **CHOL**; 511 mg **SODIUM**; 45 g **CARB**; 2 g **FIBER**; 13 g **PRO**

Lemony Fettuccine Alfredo with Shrimp and Peas: Prepare as above, except add 8 ounces peeled, deveined uncooked shrimp and 1 cup frozen peas to pasta the last 1 minute of cooking. Stir 1 teaspoon finely shredded lemon peel and 1 tablespoon lemon juice into sauce before adding pasta.

PER SERVING 603 **CAL**; 33 g **FAT** (20 g **SAT**); 192 mg **CHOL**; 634 mg **SODIUM**; 51 g **CARB**; 4 g **FIBER**; 26 g **PRO**

Shiitake Fettuccine Alfredo: Prepare as above, except cook 1½ cups sliced shiitake or button mushrooms in the butter for 4 to 5 minutes or until tender before adding the cream, salt, and pepper.

PER SERVING 544 **CAL**; 32 g **FAT** (19 g **SAT**); 106 mg **CHOL**; 513 mg **SODIUM**; 53 g **CARB**; 3 g **FIBER**; 13 g **PRO**

CHAPTER 4

cook it
slowly

Family-friendly meals ready and waiting at the end of your busy day.

CONFETTI WHITE CHILI

BEEF

Pasta Puttanesca with Beef, 83

Pot Roast Paprikash, 80

Texas Beef with Butternut Squash, 83

PORK

Hungarian Pork Goulash, 76

Kapusta Pork, 79

Southern-Style Ribs, 80

Vietnamese Pork, 77

MEATLESS

Cheesy Vegetable Alfredo, 89

CHICKEN AND TURKEY

Confetti White Chili, 86

Coq au Vin, 85

Greek Braised Chicken Legs, 86

Italian Braised Chicken with Fennel
and Cannellini, 84

Turkey Reubens, 88

Hungarian Pork Goulash

"Goulash" is an English adaptation of a Hungarian word meaning "huntsmen", and describes the chunky, meat-filled dish that hunters might prepare.

MAKES 6 servings **PREP** 30 minutes **SLOW COOK** 5 hours (low) or 2½ hours (high) + 30 minutes (high)

- 1   1½- to 2-pound pork sirloin roast
- 1   tablespoon Hungarian paprika or Spanish paprika
- 1   teaspoon caraway seeds, crushed
- ½   teaspoon garlic powder
- ½   teaspoon black pepper
- ¼   teaspoon salt
- 1   tablespoon canola oil
- 1   cup thinly sliced celery (2 stalks)
- 1   cup thinly sliced carrots (2 medium)
- 2   medium parsnips, halved lengthwise if large and thinly sliced (1 cup)
- 1   cup chopped onion (1 large)
- 1   14.5-ounce can no-salt-added diced tomatoes, undrained
- ½   cup water
- 2   cups dried wide whole grain noodles (4 ounces)
- 6   tablespoons light sour cream
      Paprika (optional)

1 Trim fat from roast. Cut roast into 2-inch cubes. In a large bowl combine paprika, caraway seeds, garlic powder, pepper, and salt. Add pork cubes and toss to coat. In a large skillet cook pork, half at a time, in hot oil over medium heat until browned, turning occasionally. Transfer pork to a 3½- or 4-quart slow cooker. Add celery, carrots, parsnips, onion, and tomatoes. Pour the water over all in cooker.

2 Cover and cook on low-heat setting for 5 to 6 hours or on high-heat setting for 2½ to 3 hours.

3 If using low-heat setting, turn to high-heat setting. Stir noodles into pork mixture in cooker. Cover and cook on high-heat setting for 30 minutes more or until noodles are tender, stirring once halfway through cooking. Top each serving with 1 tablespoon sour cream. If desired, sprinkle each serving with paprika.

PER SERVING 285 **CAL**; 9 g **FAT** (2 g **SAT**); 82 mg **CHOL**; 234 mg **SODIUM**; 24 g **CARB**; 5 g **FIBER**; 28 g **PRO**

Vietnamese Pork

Saigon meets Sonora in this fabulous sandwich wrap. Fish sauce—essential to the intriguing flavors of Vietnamese dishes—is most often shelved with other Asian staples in your supermarket.

MAKES 6 servings   **PREP** 25 minutes   **CHILL** 8 hours   **SLOW COOK** 10 hours (low) or 5 hours (high)

2   jalapeños (see note, page 15)
1   2½- to 3-pound boneless pork shoulder roast
2   tablespoons packed brown sugar
½   teaspoon black pepper
1   medium onion, cut into thin wedges
2   cloves garlic, minced
¼   cup water
2   tablespoons fish sauce
2   tablespoons lime juice
8   whole wheat flour tortillas, softened*
4   cups mesclun
1   cup halved cucumber slices
1   recipe Pickled Carrots
¼   cup snipped fresh cilantro

1 Cut one of the jalapeños in half lengthwise. Thinly slice the remaining jalapeño; wrap and chill sliced pepper until ready to serve.

2 Trim fat from meat. If necessary, cut meat to fit into a 3½- or 4-quart slow cooker. For rub, in a small bowl stir together brown sugar and pepper. Sprinkle rub evenly over meat; rub in with your fingers. Place meat in the cooker. Add halved jalapeño, onion, and garlic. In a small bowl stir together the water, fish sauce, and lime juice. Pour over mixture in cooker.

3 Cover and cook on low-heat setting for 10 to 12 hours or on high-heat setting for 5 to 6 hours.

4 Using a slotted spoon, remove meat and onion from cooker; discard cooking liquid. Using two forks, pull meat apart into shreds. Stir onion into shredded meat.

5 For each serving, spoon ⅔ cup of the shredded meat mixture onto a tortilla. Top with mesclun, cucumber, Pickled Carrots, cilantro, and sliced jalapeño.

***Note:** Place tortillas between paper towels. Microwave on high for 20 to 40 seconds.

Pickled Carrots: In a glass bowl stir together ½ cup warm water, 2 tablespoons white vinegar, 1 tablespoon sugar, and ½ teaspoon salt. Add 1 cup carrots cut into thin bite-size strips (2 medium). Cover and chill for 8 hours before serving. Store in the refrigerator for up to 1 week.

PER SERVING 362 **CAL**; 7 g **FAT** (2 g **SAT**); 85 mg **CHOL**; 966 mg **SODIUM**; 36 g **CARB**; 3 g **FIBER**; 37 g **PRO**

Kapusta Pork

Frequent recipe contest contestant Linda Cifuentes, a nurse from Mahomet, Illinois, dug up her Czech family roots to come up with the blend of eastern European flavors that earned her the title of Crock Star in the 2010 National Pork Board's Crocktoberfest recipe contest. She thanks her husband for suggesting beer as the ingredient that put her recipe into the winner's circle. As a finalist she was flown to New York City, where she wined and dined with celebrity chefs and food bloggers. Her top prize awarded by the president of the Pork Board was $5,000, a year's supply of slow cooker liners, and $500 worth of pork donated to her local food bank.

MAKES 8 servings **PREP** 30 minutes **SLOW COOK** 5 hours (high)

3 **pounds boneless pork loin**

3 **cloves garlic, halved lengthwise**
   Salt and black pepper

12 **ounces sliced bacon, chopped**

4 **cups shredded cabbage**

1 **14.5-ounce can sauerkraut**

1 **28-ounce can diced tomatoes**

1 **tablespoon caraway seeds**

2 **bay leaves**

8 **ounces German beer (Pilsner)**

1 With a sharp knife, make 6 small slits in the pork loin. Insert garlic slices into the slits. Season to taste with salt and pepper.

2 Place pork in a 6-quart slow cooker. Add bacon, cabbage, sauerkraut, undrained tomatoes, caraway seeds, bay leaves, and beer. Cover and cook on high-heat setting for 5 to 6 hours. Remove bay leaves.

3 Transfer meat to a cutting board. Use forks to shred the meat; place in a bowl. Skim fat from cooking liquid. Serve cooking liquid and cabbage mixture with the shredded pork.

PER SERVING 540 **CAL**; 35 g **FAT** (12 g **SAT**); 146 mg **CHOL**; 1,113 mg **SODIUM**; 10 g **CARB**; 4 g **FIBER**; 42 g **PRO**

Southern-Style Ribs

If you think that pork ribs like these—sensational, spicy, and succulent—had to be prepared over a low live fire, think again. Your trusty slow cooker will surprise you with its barbecue ability.

MAKES 6 to 8 servings **PREP** 25 minutes
SLOW COOK 8 hours (low) or 4 hours (high)
BROIL 5 minutes

4	to 5 pounds pork loin back ribs or meaty pork spareribs, cut into 2- to 3-rib portions
1	tablespoon smoked paprika or sweet paprika
1½	teaspoons packed brown sugar
1	teaspoon ground pasilla chile pepper or ancho chile pepper
½	teaspoon salt
½	teaspoon garlic powder
½	teaspoon ground coriander
½	teaspoon dry mustard
¼	teaspoon celery salt
¼	teaspoon coarsely ground black pepper
⅛	teaspoon cayenne pepper
¾	cup barbecue sauce
½	cup chicken broth

1 Trim fat from ribs. For rub, in a small bowl combine paprika, brown sugar, ground pasilla pepper, salt, garlic powder, coriander, dry mustard, celery salt, black pepper, and cayenne pepper. Generously sprinkle rub over both sides of ribs; rub in with your fingers. Place ribs in a 5- to 6-quart slow cooker, cutting to fit.

2 In a small bowl combine ¼ cup of the barbecue sauce and the broth; pour over ribs.

3 Cover and cook on low-heat setting for 8 to 10 hours or on high-heat setting for 4 to 5 hours.

4 Preheat broiler. Line a baking sheet with foil. Transfer ribs, meaty sides up, to the prepared baking sheet. Brush with the remaining ½ cup barbecue sauce. Broil 6 to 8 inches from the heat for 5 to 8 minutes or until sauce begins to brown.

PER SERVING 584 **CAL**; 44 g **FAT** (16 g **SAT**); 152 mg **CHOL**; 831 mg **SODIUM**; 13 g **CARB**; 0 g **FIBER**; 30 g **PRO**

Pot Roast Paprikash

Slow-cooked beef rump roast emerges from the slow cooker ready to shred into tender, moist morsels for slathering over hot buttered noodles.

MAKES 8 servings **PREP** 25 minutes
SLOW COOK 10 hours (low) or 5 hours (high)
+ 30 minutes (high)

1	2½-pound beef rump roast
2	tablespoons paprika
½	teaspoon smoked paprika
1	14.5-ounce can diced tomatoes, undrained
1	14.5-ounce can beef broth
3	medium onions, halved and cut into ½-inch slices
3	large carrots, coarsely chopped
1	12-ounce jar roasted red sweet peppers, drained and cut into ½-inch-wide strips
¼	cup water
2	tablespoons cornstarch
1	8-ounce carton sour cream
	Salt and black pepper
2	cups dried medium noodles (4 ounces)
¼	cup butter
⅓	cup snipped fresh parsley

1 Trim fat from meat; cut meat into four pieces. Place meat in a 4- to 5-quart slow cooker. In a small bowl combine paprika and smoked paprika. Sprinkle paprika mixture over beef. Top with tomatoes, broth, onions, carrots, and sweet peppers.

2 Cover and cook on low-heat setting for 10 to 12 hours or on high-heat setting for 5 to 6 hours.

3 Using tongs, transfer meat to a cutting board. Use two forks to pull meat apart into coarse shreds. Skim fat from cooking liquid. Stir meat back into cooker. Set cooker on high-heat setting. In a small bowl whisk together the water and cornstarch; stir into meat in cooker. Cover and cook for 30 minutes more. Stir in sour cream. Season to taste with salt and black pepper.

4 Meanwhile, cook noodles according to package directions; drain. Toss with butter. Serve roast over noodles. Sprinkle with parsley.

PER SERVING 523 **CAL**; 28 g **FAT** (13 g **SAT**); 136 mg **CHOL**; 590 mg **SODIUM**; 35 g **CARB**; 4 g **FIBER**; 34 g **PRO**

POT ROAST PAPRIKASH

TEXAS BEEF WITH BUTTERNUT SQUASH

Texas Beef with Butternut Squash

Two teaspoons of unsweetened cocoa is the secret to the full-bodied flavor of this remarkable, ready-when-you-are Southwestern-style stew.

MAKES 8 servings **PREP** 25 minutes
SLOW COOK 8 hours (low) or 4 hours (high)

- 1½ **pounds beef chuck roast**
- 4 **cups 1½-inch cubes peeled butternut squash**
- 2 **14.5-ounce cans fire-roasted diced tomatoes, undrained**
- 1½ **cups no-salt-added beef broth or water**
- ¾ **cup chopped onion**
- 1 **4-ounce can diced green chiles**
- 1 **tablespoon ground ancho chile pepper**
- 2 **teaspoons unsweetened cocoa powder**
- 1 **teaspoon ground cumin**
- 1 **teaspoon dried oregano, crushed**
- 3 **cloves garlic, minced**
  Snipped fresh cilantro
  Hot cooked polenta or hot cooked rice (optional)

1 Trim beef roast and cut beef into 2-inch pieces. In a 5- to 6-quart slow cooker stir together beef, squash, tomatoes, beef broth, onion, chiles, chile pepper, cocoa powder, cumin, oregano, and garlic.

2 Cover and cook on low-heat setting for 8 to 10 hours or on high-heat setting for 4 to 5 hours. Sprinkle each serving with cilantro. If desired, serve with polenta or hot cooked rice.

PER SERVING 258 **CAL**; 13 g **FAT** (5 g **SAT**); 75 mg **CHOL**; 313 mg **SODIUM**; 16 g **CARB**; 4 g **FIBER**; 19 g **PRO**

Pasta Puttanesca with Beef

Chopped anchovy imbues the robust pasta sauce with delightful depth of flavor and sensational savory notes. Should you wish, however, you may achieve a pretty close match by substituting about a tablespoon of anchovy paste.

MAKES 8 servings **PREP** 25 minutes **COOK** 15 minutes
SLOW COOK 4 hours (low) or 2 hours (high)

- 1 **pound 90% or higher lean ground beef**
- ¾ **cup chopped onion**
- 4 **cloves garlic, minced**
- 2 **14.5-ounce cans no-salt-added diced tomatoes, undrained**
- 1 **6-ounce can no-salt-added tomato paste**
- 3 **anchovy fillets, chopped**
- 1 **teaspoon dried oregano, crushed**
- ¼ **teaspoon crushed red pepper**
- 8 **ounces dried multigrain penne pasta (about 2½ cups)**
- ¼ **cup chopped kalamata olives**
- ¼ **cup snipped fresh parsley**
  Snipped fresh parsley (optional)

1 In a large nonstick skillet cook ground beef, onion, and garlic over medium heat until meat browns and onion is tender. Drain off and discard fat.

2 In a 3½- or 4-quart slow cooker combine beef mixture, tomatoes, tomato paste, anchovies, oregano, and crushed red pepper.

3 Cover and cook on low-heat setting for 4 to 6 hours or on high-heat setting for 2 to 3 hours.

4 Cook pasta according to package directions; drain. Stir olives and ¼ cup parsley into cooker. Serve puttanesca over hot cooked pasta. If desired, garnish with additional snipped fresh parsley.

PER SERVING 262 **CAL**; 8 g **FAT** (2 g **SAT**); 38 mg **CHOL**; 215 mg **SODIUM**; 30 g **CARB**; 5 g **FIBER**; 19 g **PRO**

Italian Braised Chicken with Fennel and Cannellini

Flavor-packed chicken dark meat cuts—such as the drumsticks and thighs chosen for this recipe—are made tender and succulent by the gentle braising that the slow cooker provides.

MAKES 6 servings **PREP** 30 minutes **SLOW COOK** 5 hours (low) or 2½ hours (high)

- **2** to 2½ pounds chicken drumsticks and/or thighs, skin removed
- **¾** teaspoon salt
- **¼** teaspoon black pepper
- **1** 15-ounce can cannellini beans, rinsed and drained
- **1** bulb fennel, cored and cut into thin wedges
- **1** medium yellow sweet pepper, seeded and cut into 1-inch pieces
- **1** medium onion, cut into thin wedges
- **3** cloves garlic, minced
- **1** teaspoon snipped fresh rosemary or ½ teaspoon dried rosemary
- **1** teaspoon snipped fresh oregano or ½ teaspoon dried oregano
- **¼** teaspoon crushed red pepper
- **1** 14.5-ounce can diced tomatoes, undrained
- **½** cup dry white wine or reduced-sodium chicken broth
- **¼** cup tomato paste
- **¼** cup shaved Parmesan cheese
- **1** tablespoon snipped fresh parsley

1 Sprinkle chicken pieces with ¼ teaspoon of the salt and the black pepper. Place chicken in a 3½- or 4-quart slow cooker. Top with beans, fennel, sweet pepper, onion, garlic, rosemary, oregano, and crushed red pepper. In a medium bowl combine tomatoes, white wine, tomato paste, and remaining ½ teaspoon salt; pour over mixture in cooker.

2 Cover and cook on low-heat setting for 5 to 6 hours or on high-heat setting for 2½ to 3 hours.

3 Sprinkle each serving with Parmesan cheese and parsley.

PER SERVING 223 **CAL**; 4 g **FAT** (1 g **SAT**); 68 mg **CHOL**; 762 mg **SODIUM**; 23 g **CARB**; 7 g **FIBER**; 25 g **PRO**

Coq au Vin

This classic French dish is typically prepared by braising the chicken in red wine. This recipe calls for a bit of red wine vinegar instead. The vinegar adds the mellow flavor of red wine without changing the color of the chicken thighs.

MAKES 6 servings **PREP** 35 minutes **SLOW COOK** 5 hours (low) or 2½ hours (high)

- **1** 8-ounce package fresh mushrooms, halved (or quartered if large)
- **4** medium carrots, cut into ¼-inch slices
- **1½** cups frozen pearl onions
  Nonstick cooking spray
- **6** chicken thighs, skinned (2¼ to 2½ pounds total)
- **½** teaspoon salt
- **½** teaspoon black pepper
- **1** cup dry red wine or reduced-sodium chicken broth
- **½** cup reduced-sodium chicken broth
- **2** tablespoons tapioca
- **2** tablespoons red wine vinegar
- **1½** teaspoons herbes de Provence
- **3** cloves garlic, minced
- **2** tablespoons snipped fresh parsley
- **3** cups hot cooked whole grain wide noodles

1 In a 4- to 5-quart slow cooker combine mushrooms, carrots, and onions. Set aside.

2 Lightly coat a large unheated nonstick skillet with cooking spray; heat over medium-high heat. Sprinkle both sides of chicken thighs with ¼ teaspoon of the salt and ¼ teaspoon of the pepper. Add chicken thighs to skillet, meaty sides down. Cook about 6 minutes or until browned, turning once. Add chicken to cooker.

3 Add wine to skillet; bring to boiling. Reduce heat; simmer for 2 minutes, using a wooden spoon to scrape up browned bits from bottom and sides of skillet. Remove from heat. Stir in broth, tapioca, vinegar, herbes de Provence, garlic, the remaining ¼ teaspoon salt, and the remaining ¼ teaspoon pepper. Pour over chicken in cooker.

4 Cover and cook on low-heat setting for 5 to 5½ hours or on high-heat setting for 2½ to 2¾ hours. To serve, sprinkle with parsley and serve with noodles.

PER SERVING 295 **CAL**; 5 g **FAT** (1 g **SAT**); 80 mg **CHOL**; 365 mg **SODIUM**; 33 g **CARB**; 5 g **FIBER**; 25 g **PRO**

Greek Braised Chicken Legs

To skin chicken legs easily, grasp the skin on the chubby end with a dry paper towel and pull back toward the bone. The paper towel will give traction on slippery chicken skin.

MAKES 4 servings **PREP** 25 minutes
SLOW COOK 6 hours (low) or 3 hours (high)

1	medium onion, sliced
8	chicken drumsticks (about 2¾ pounds total), skinned
1	teaspoon Greek seasoning
3	cups halved grape tomatoes or cherry tomatoes
¼	cup chopped pimiento-stuffed green olives
4	cloves garlic, minced
2	cups hot cooked brown rice
¼	cup snipped fresh parsley or parsley sprigs
1	teaspoon finely shredded lemon peel

1 Place onion in a 3½- or 4-quart slow cooker. Sprinkle drumsticks with Greek seasoning. Place drumsticks on top of onion in cooker. Top drumsticks with tomatoes, olives, and garlic.

2 Cover and cook on low-heat setting for 6 to 8 hours or on high-heat setting for 3 to 4 hours.

3 Using a slotted spoon, serve chicken over hot cooked brown rice. If desired, spoon some of the cooking liquid over top. Sprinkle with parsley and lemon peel.

PER SERVING 404 **CAL**; 9 g **FAT** (2 g **SAT**); 157 mg **CHOL**; 338 mg **SODIUM**; 32 g **CARB**; 4 g **FIBER**; 46 g **PRO**

Confetti White Chili

"Confetti" is an apt description for this chicken and white bean chili—it's strewn with colorful little bits of chopped sweet peppers and carrots.

MAKES 6 to 8 servings **PREP** 25 minutes
SLOW COOK 6 hours (low) or 3 hours (high)
+ 15 minutes (high)

3	15-ounce can Great Northern, pinto, or cannellini beans, rinsed and drained
1½	cups chopped red, green, and/or yellow sweet peppers
1	cup coarsely shredded carrot
½	cup sliced green onions
1	jalapeño, seeded and minced (see note, page 15) (optional)
2	garlic, minced
2	teaspoons dried oregano, crushed
1½	teaspoons ground cumin
½	teaspoon salt
2	14.5-ounce cans chicken broth
2½	cups shredded cooked chicken
	Shredded Monterey Jack cheese (optional)

1 Place 2 cans of beans in a 3½- or 4-quart slow cooker. Use a potato masher or fork to mash beans. Stir in remaining beans, sweet peppers, carrot, green onions, jalapeño if using, garlic, oregano, cumin, and salt. Add broth. Stir until well combined.

2 Cover; cook on low-heat setting for 6 to 8 hours or on high-heat setting for 3 to 4 hours. If using low-heat setting, turn to high-heat setting. Stir chicken into chili. Cover; cook for 15 minutes more or until chicken is heated through.

3 Spoon chili into bowls. If desired, sprinkle each serving with cheese.

PER SERVING 407 **CAL**; 6 g **FAT** (1 g **SAT**); 53 mg **CHOL**; 800 mg **SODIUM**; 54 g **CARB**; 13 g **FIBER**; 35 g **PRO**

CONFETTI WHITE CHILI

Turkey Reubens

All of the flavors that make the Reuben such a beloved sandwich slowly in the slow cooker. When you're ready, all that's left to do is shred the tender turkey and pile the amazing mixture over slices of cheese-topped toasted rye bread.

MAKES 6 servings **PREP** 15 minutes **SLOW COOK** 7 hours (low) or 3½ hours (high) + 30 minutes (high) **BROIL** 2 minutes

- **2 stalks celery, cut crosswise into thirds**
- **1 medium onion, cut into wedges**
- **1 cup water**
- **½ teaspoon caraway seeds, crushed**
- **¼ teaspoon celery seeds**
- **¼ teaspoon salt**
- **¼ teaspoon black pepper**
- **2 to 2½ pounds bone-in turkey breast halves**
- **6 cups shredded fresh cabbage**
- **2 cups purchased coarsely shredded carrots**
- **6 slices rye bread**
- **6 ¾-ounce slices reduced-fat Swiss cheese**
- **½ cup bottled reduced-calorie Thousand Island salad dressing**

1 Place celery and onion in a 3½- or 4-quart slow cooker. Add the water to cooker. In a small bowl combine caraway seeds, celery seeds, salt, and pepper. Sprinkle evenly over turkey. Place turkey on celery and onions in cooker.

2 Cover and cook on low-heat setting for 7 to 8 hours or on high-heat setting for 3½ to 4 hours. If using low-heat setting, turn to high-heat setting. Add cabbage and carrots to cooker; cover and cook for 30 minutes more.

3 Preheat broiler. Using tongs, remove cabbage and carrots from cooker; set aside. Transfer turkey to a cutting board; remove and discard skin. Thinly slice or shred turkey. Discard celery and onion from cooker. Place bread slices on a large baking sheet. Broil 3 to 4 inches from the heat for 1 to 2 minutes or until tops are lightly toasted. Turn bread slices over and top each with a slice of cheese. Broil 1 to 2 minutes more or until cheese is melted.

4 Place ¾ cup turkey and ¾ cup cabbage mixture on each cheese-topped bread slice. Top each open-face sandwich with about 1 tablespoon of the salad dressing.

PER SERVING 341 **CAL**; 8 g **FAT** (3 g **SAT**); 86 mg **CHOL**; 591 mg **SODIUM**; 28 g **CARB**; 4 g **FIBER**; 41 g **PRO**

Cheesy Vegetable Alfredo

The decision is yours. Serve this cheesy, veggie-packed dish as a luxurious, meat-free side dish or in smaller portions as an amazing accompaniment to marinated beef.

MAKES 6 servings **PREP** 25 minutes **SLOW COOK** 5 hours (low) or 2 hours (high) **STAND** 5 minutes

8	ounces fresh green beans, trimmed and halved crosswise
2	cups fresh button or cremini mushrooms, sliced
½	medium head cauliflower, cut into large florets
1	9-ounce package frozen artichoke hearts, thawed
1	cup thinly sliced carrots (2 medium)
1	cup chopped onion (1 medium)
1	cup fat-free evaporated milk
1	5- to 6.5-ounce container light semisoft cheese with garlic and fine herbs
1	cup shredded Parmesan cheese (4 ounces)
6	ounces dried whole grain linguine
1	cup cherry tomatoes, quartered or halved
	Shredded fresh basil

1 In a 4- to 5-quart slow cooker combine green beans, mushrooms, cauliflower, artichoke hearts, carrots, and onion. Pour evaporated milk over all in cooker.

2 Cover and cook on low-heat setting for 5 to 5½ hours or on high-heat setting for 2 to 2½ hours.

3 Add semisoft cheese and Parmesan cheese to cooker. Cover and let stand for 5 minutes. Stir gently until cheese is melted. Meanwhile, cook linguine according to package directions; drain. Add linguine to cooker and toss to coat. Divide Alfredo among six serving plates. Top each serving with tomatoes and basil.

PER SERVING 343 **CAL**; 11 g **FAT** (7 g **SAT**); 31 mg **CHOL**; 547 mg **SODIUM**; 39 g **CARB**; 9 g **FIBER**; 19 g **PRO**

CHAPTER 5
great grilling

Turn the page to discover the exhilarating thrill of the grill.

BISON BURGERS WITH
CARAMELIZED DATES AND ONIONS

BEEF

Cuban Burgers, 99

Spice-Rubbed Beef Tenderloin, 100

Steak Remoulade Sandwiches, 100

CHICKEN

Chicken-Apple Burgers, 103

Grillers Stuffed with Spinach and Smoked Gouda, 105

Spicy Buffalo Chicken Salad, 105

BISON

Bison Burgers with Caramelized Dates
and Onions, 102

FISH AND SEAFOOD

Fish Sandwiches with Red Pepper-Onion Relish, 106

Salmon Caesar Salad, 106

Shrimp Po' Boy with Dried Tomato Aïoli, 108

Zucchini Crab Cakes, 109

PORK

Baconista Brats, 98

Campfire Ham 'n' Swiss Dijon Potato Packet, 97

Maple-Apricot Pork Medallions, 92

Pork Chops Stuffed with Blue Cheese, 92

Taste of Dole Pork Sliders, 95

Pork Chops Stuffed with Blue Cheese

A mere 20 minutes' prep time makes these company-special stuffed chops doable even on a busy weeknight. Add a simple green salad and crusty bread and you're good to go.

MAKES 4 servings **PREP** 20 minutes **GRILL** 12 minutes

- ⅓ cup shredded carrot (1 large)
- ⅓ cup crumbled blue cheese
- ¼ cup chopped pecans
- 2 tablespoons thinly sliced green onion (1)
- 1 teaspoon Worcestershire sauce
- 4 bone-in pork loin chops or pork rib chops, cut 1¼ inches thick (about 2¼ pounds)
  Barbecue sauce
  Crumbled blue cheese (optional)

1 For stuffing, in a small bowl combine carrot, the ⅓ cup cheese, pecans, green onion, and Worcestershire sauce. Set aside.

2 Trim fat from chops. Make a pocket in each chop by cutting horizontally from the fat side almost to the bone. Spoon one-fourth of the stuffing into each pocket. Secure the openings with wooden toothpicks.

3 For a charcoal grill, arrange medium-hot coals around a drip pan. Test for medium heat above the pan. Place chops on the grill rack over pan. Cover and grill for 12 to 16 minutes or until chops are slightly pink in center (145°F), turning once and brushing frequently with barbecue sauce during the last 10 minutes of grilling. Allow chops to rest for at least 3 minutes. (For a gas grill, preheat grill. Reduce heat to medium. Adjust for indirect cooking. Place chops on grill rack over the burner that is turned off. Grill as directed.) Remove toothpicks.

4 To serve, sprinkle chops with additional cheese if desired.

PER SERVING 406 **CAL**; 27 g **FAT** (9 g **SAT**); 106 mg **CHOL**; 272 mg **SODIUM**; 3 g **CARB**; 1 g **FIBER**; 37 g **PRO**

Maple-Apricot Pork Medallions

When using maple syrup in recipes—such as this one—in which maple flavor is a key component, splurge on pure maple syrup. It's a bit pricey but provides authentic flavor that maple-flavor pancake syrups lack.

MAKES 6 servings **PREP** 30 minutes **GRILL** 20 minutes

- 2 12-ounce pork tenderloins
- 15 to 20 slices bacon*
- 2 tablespoons finely chopped shallot (1 medium)
- 2 tablespoons butter
- ⅔ cup coarsely snipped dried apricots
- ⅓ cup apricot vinegar, other light-color fruit-flavor vinegar, or champagne vinegar
- 2 teaspoons finely shredded orange peel
  Dash ground allspice
  Dash black pepper
- ¼ cup orange liqueur or orange juice
- ½ cup maple syrup

1 Trim fat from pork. Cut pork crosswise into 1½-inch slices (save the thin end portions for another use). In a large skillet cook bacon over medium heat just until lightly browned but not fully cooked. Remove bacon and drain on paper towels. Wrap a slice of bacon around each slice of pork; secure with a wooden toothpick.

2 For a charcoal grill, grill pork slices on the rack of an uncovered grill directly over medium coals for 15 to 20 minutes or until pork is slightly pink in center and juices run clear (145°F), turning once halfway through grilling. Allow slices to rest at least 3 minutes. (For a gas grill, preheat grill. Reduce heat to medium. Place pork slices on grill rack over heat. Cover and grill as above.)

3 Meanwhile, for sauce, in a medium saucepan cook shallot in hot butter over medium heat for 1 minute. Add dried apricots, vinegar, orange peel, allspice, and pepper. Stir in liqueur. Bring to boiling; reduce heat. Simmer, uncovered, for 8 to 10 minutes or until sauce is thickened. Stir in maple syrup; heat through.

4 To serve medallions, remove and discard toothpicks. Serve with warm sauce.

****Note:** Use 1 slice of bacon for each medallion.

PER SERVING 398 **CAL**; 16 g **FAT** (7 g **SAT**); 104 mg **CHOL**; 354 mg **SODIUM**; 31 g **CARB**; 1 g **FIBER**; 31 g **PRO**

PORK CHOPS STUFFED WITH BLUE CHEESE

Taste of Dole Pork Sliders

Competing in recipe contests has paid off handsomely for Jeanette Nelson, whose recipe for pork sliders garnered First Place honors in the Dole California Cook-Off. Jeanette, a young Bridgeport, West Virginia, mother won a total of $60,000 and 10 all-expenses-paid trips in 2012—a windfall that not only allowed her to be a stay-at-home mom, but also provided the means by which her husband—a coal miner—was able to return to school to pursue his dream of becoming a physician's assistant.

MAKES 12 servings **PREP** 50 minutes **GRILL** 6 minutes

1	20-ounce can Dole Pineapple Tidbits
¾	cup mayonnaise with olive oil
2	cloves garlic, minced
¾	cup Dole frozen mango chunks, partially thawed
2	teaspoons toasted ground ginger*
1¾	teaspoons coarse sea salt
¼	teaspoon freshly ground black pepper
¾	cup julienned jicama
½	cup plus 2 tablespoons coarsely chopped cilantro
2	pounds lean ground pork
1	teaspoon toasted ground cumin*
½	teaspoon red pepper flakes
½	cup Island teriyaki sauce
12	Hawaiian sweet dinner rolls

1 Preheat gas grill with lid closed to medium-high heat. Drain pineapple tidbits, reserving 3 tablespoons juice.

2 For ginger-pineapple-mango mayonnaise, in a food processor combine mayonnaise, ⅓ cup of the tidbits, 1 clove minced garlic, ½ cup of the mango chunks, and 1 teaspoon of the toasted ground ginger. Cover and process until smooth. Season to taste with salt and black pepper.

3 Finely chop remaining pineapple tidbits and mangoes; set aside. For pineapple-jicama salsa, in a medium bowl combine ¾ cup of the finely chopped pineapple tidbits, jicama, and ½ cup of the cilantro; mix well. Season with ¼ teaspoon of the salt and the ¼ teaspoon black pepper.

4 In a large bowl combine pork, reserved pineapple juice, ¼ cup of the finely chopped pineapple tidbits, finely chopped mango, toasted ground cumin, red pepper flakes, ¼ cup teriyaki sauce, the remaining 1½ teaspoons salt, remaining garlic, remaining ginger, and 2 tablespoons cilantro just until mixed. Divide mixture into 12 equal portions and shape into 3½-inch-wide patties. Cover and refrigerate until ready to grill.

5 Brush grill rack with vegetable oil. Place patties on rack; cover and cook 3 to 5 minutes on each side, turning once, until pork is fully cooked (145°F). During the last few minutes of grilling, baste patties with remaining teriyaki sauce. Place buns, cut sides down, on rack to lightly toast.

6 Spread cut sides of buns with the ginger-pineapple-mango mayonnaise. Place a patty on each bun bottom; top with pineapple-jicama salsa. Add bun tops and serve.

*Note: To toast ground spices, place in a small heavy skillet (cast iron is ideal) over medium heat. Toast, stirring constantly, until fragrant. Immediately empty the spices into a bowl and stir them to stop the cooking.

PER SERVING 385 **CAL**; 20 g **FAT** (6 g **SAT**); 73 mg **CHOL**; 520 mg **SODIUM**; 32 g **CARB**; 2 g **FIBER**; 18 g **PRO**

Campfire Ham 'n' Swiss Dijon Potato Packet

Cara Firestone—a singer and avid camper—came up with the winning entry in the 2012 Gather-Around-the-Campfire recipe contest sponsored by the Wisconsin Potato and Vegetable Growers' Association. Her impetus? Create a recipe that would appeal to her her two young adventurous sons and husband. Lauded by judges for its "ease of preparation and culinary creativity," her campfire-baked foil packet recipe also won the most online consumer votes, winning the Austin, Texas, cook a Guide Series campsite canopy.

MAKES 2 servings **PREP** 20 minutes **GRILL** 25 minutes

Nonstick cooking spray
1   **large Wisconsin potato, cubed**
1   **tablespoon minced onion**
⅓   **cup diced ham**
2   **tablespoons sour cream**
1   **teaspoon Dijon mustard**
¼   **cup seasoned croutons (optional)**
¼   **cup grated Swiss cheese**

1 Fold a 36 x 18-inch sheet of heavy foil in half to make an 18-inch square. Coat foil with cooking spray. Place potato, onion, and ham in center of foil.

2 In a small bowl stir together the sour cream and mustard; spoon over the ham. If desired, top with croutons. Bring up two opposite edges of foil; seal with a double fold. Fold remaining edges to completely enclose vegetables, leaving space for steam to build.

3 For a charcoal grill, grill packet on the rack of an uncovered grill directly over medium coals for 25 minutes or until potatoes are tender, turning packet occasionally. (For a gas grill, preheat grill. Reduce heat to medium. Place packet on a grill rack over heat. Cover and grill as directed.)

4 Carefully open packet (sour cream mixture may appear curdled); sprinkle potatoes with cheese. Loosely pinch packet together; let stand about 2 minutes or until cheese is melted.

PER SERVING 198 **CAL**; 9 g **FAT** (5 g **SAT**); 34 mg **CHOL**; 400 mg **SODIUM**; 19 g **CARB**; 2 g **FIBER**; 10 g **PRO**

Baconista Brats

If you like to try new things, pop a tin of smoked paprika in your cart the next time you go shopping. Made from smoke-dried red peppers, the powder adds another layer of sweet smokiness to this—and many other—recipes.

MAKES 5 servings **PREP** 30 minutes **MARINATE** 6 hours **COOK** 10 minutes **GRILL** 5 minutes

5 uncooked bratwurst links or turkey bratwurst (about 1 pound)

1 12-ounce can dark German beer, desired beer, or 1½ cups beef broth

½ cup coarsely chopped onion (1 medium)

3 tablespoons bottled steak sauce

2½ teaspoons smoked paprika or sweet paprika

4 cloves garlic, coarsely chopped

5 slices uncooked bacon

5 round hard rolls, bratwursts buns, hoagie buns, or other crusty rolls, split and toasted

1 recipe Tangy Midwest Slaw

1 Use the tines of a fork to pierce the skin of each bratwurst several times. Place bratwurst in a large resealable plastic bag set in a shallow dish. For marinade, stir together beer, onion, steak sauce, paprika, and garlic. Pour over bratwurst; seal bag. Marinate in the refrigerator for 6 to 24 hours, turning bag occasionally.

2 Transfer bratwurst and marinade to a large saucepan. Bring to boiling; reduce heat. Cover and simmer for 10 minutes.

3 Meanwhile, in a large skillet cook bacon until browned but not crisp. Drain on paper towels.

4 Using tongs, remove bratwurst from saucepan; discard marinade. Let bratwurst cool slightly. Wrap a slice of bacon around each bratwurst; secure with wooden toothpicks.

5 For a charcoal grill, grill bratwurst on the rack of an uncovered grill directly over medium coals about 5 minutes or until browned and bacon is crisp, turning often. (For a gas grill, preheat grill. Reduce heat to medium. Grill bratwurst on grill rack over heat. Cover; grill as directed.)

6 Remove and discard toothpicks from bratwurst. Serve bratwurst on rolls with Tangy Midwest Slaw.

Tangy Midwest Slaw: In a medium bowl combine ⅓ cup mayonnaise, 1 tablespoon rice vinegar or white wine vinegar, 1 tablespoon sweet pickle juice, ¼ teaspoon celery seeds, and ⅛ teaspoon bottled hot pepper sauce. Add 2½ cups packaged shredded cabbage with carrot (coleslaw mix) or half of a small head green cabbage, shredded. Toss to coat. Makes about 2 cups.

PER SERVING 682 **CAL**; 48 g **FAT** (10 g **SAT**); 103 mg **CHOL**; 1,601 mg **SODIUM**; 37 g **CARB**; 2 g **FIBER**; 23 g **PRO**

Cuban Burgers

Inspired by El Cubano—Cuba's beloved ham and pork sandwich—this burger brings Caribbean flavor to a most-American meal.

MAKES 4 servings **PREP** 25 minutes **GRILL** 14 minutes **COOK** 5 minutes

1	**pound ground beef**
4	**teaspoon garlic powder**
1	**teaspoon ground cumin**
¼	**teaspoon salt**
¼	**teaspoon black pepper**
4	**thin slices cooked ham (about 3 ounces)**
16	**slices Fontina or provolone cheese (about 3 ounces)**
4	**rolls or buns, split and toasted**
8	**whole dill pickles, sliced horizontally into 8 slices**
½	**slices red onion**
⅛	**slices tomato**
1	**recipe Mojo Sauce**

1 In a large bowl combine beef, garlic powder, cumin, salt, and pepper; mix well. Shape into four ¾-inch-thick patties.

2 For a charcoal grill, grill patties on the rack of an uncovered grill directly over medium coals for 14 to 18 minutes or until done* (160°F), turning once halfway through grilling. Add a slice of ham and cheese to each burger the last 1 minute of grilling. (For a gas grill, preheat grill. Reduce heat to medium. Place patties on grill rack over heat. Cover; grill as directed.)

3 Serve burgers on rolls with pickles, onion, and tomato. Drizzle with some of the Mojo Sauce; pass remaining sauce.

Mojo Sauce: In a medium skillet cook 6 cloves garlic, minced, in 2 tablespoons olive oil over medium heat just until they start to brown. Remove from heat. Carefully add ⅓ cup orange juice, ⅓ cup lemon juice, 1 teaspoon ground cumin, and ½ teaspoon each salt and black pepper. Bring to boiling; reduce heat. Simmer, uncovered, about 5 minutes or until slightly reduced. Remove from heat; cool. Whisk before serving.

PER SERVING 558 **CAL**; 31 g **FAT** (12 g **SAT**); 108 mg **CHOL**; 1,716 mg **SODIUM**; 32 g **CARB**; 3 g **FIBER**; 36 g **PRO**

***Note:** The internal color of a patty is not a reliable doneness indicator. A beef patty cooked to 160°F is safe, regardless of color. To measure the doneness of a patty, insert an instant-read thermometer through the side of the patty to a depth of 2 to 3 inches.

Steak Remoulade Sandwiches

Remoulade—pronounced reh-moo-lahd—is an egg-thickened or mayonnaise-based sauce common in French cookery. Here the sauce is studded with tiny sour pickles and briny capers, making it an enticing accompaniment to steak.

MAKES 4 servings **PREP** 15 minutes **GRILL** 8 minutes

- ¼ **cup light mayonnaise dressing or salad dressing**
- 1½ **teaspoons finely minced cornichons or gherkins**
- 1 **teaspoon capers, chopped**
- ¼ **teaspoon lemon juice**
  Freshly ground black pepper
- 2 **8-ounce boneless beef loin strip steaks**
- 2 **teaspoons prepared garlic spread or 2 teaspoons bottled minced garlic**
- 1 **large yellow sweet pepper, seeded and cut lengthwise into 8 strips**
- 4 **kaiser or French-style rolls, split**
- 1 **cup arugula or spinach leaves**

1 For remoulade, in a small bowl combine mayonnaise dressing, cornichons, capers, lemon juice, and a pinch of freshly ground black pepper. Cover and refrigerate.

2 Pat steaks dry with paper towels. Rub garlic spread on steaks. Sprinkle with additional freshly ground black pepper.

3 For a charcoal grill, place steaks and sweet pepper strips on rack of an uncovered grill directly over medium coals. Grill until meat is desired doneness, turning once. (Allow 8 to 12 minutes for medium doneness.) Transfer cooked steaks and sweet pepper strips to a cutting board; cut steaks into ¼-inch slices.

4 If desired, grill rolls directly over medium heat about 1 minute or until toasted. Spread remoulade on bottom halves of rolls; top with arugula, steak slices, sweet pepper, and roll tops.

PER SERVING 380 **CAL**; 13 g **FAT** (3 g **SAT**); 65 mg **CHOL**; 516 mg **SODIUM**; 37 g **CARB**; 0 g **FIBER**; 29 g **PRO**

Spice-Rubbed Beef Tenderloin

So often, simple is best. This spice-rubbed beef tenderloin proves the point—the rub, made with spice cabinet staples that blend in a matter of minutes, takes this elegant cut of beef from delicious to divine.

MAKES 12 servings **PREP** 15 minutes **GRILL** 1 hour **STAND** 15 minutes

- 1 **tablespoon chili powder**
- 1 **tablespoon ground coriander**
- 1 **tablespoon packed brown sugar**
- 1 **teaspoon paprika**
- 1 **teaspoon dry mustard**
- 1 **teaspoon salt**
- ½ **teaspoon garlic powder**
- ¼ **teaspoon cayenne pepper**
- 1 **3- to 4-pound center-cut beef tenderloin roast**

1 For rub, in a small bowl combine chili powder, coriander, brown sugar, paprika, dry mustard, salt, garlic powder, and cayenne pepper. Sprinkle rub on roast and rub in with your fingers.

2 For a charcoal grill, arrange hot coals around a drip pan. Test for medium-high heat above the pan. Place roast on grill rack over pan. Cover and grill for 60 to 75 minutes for medium-rare (135°F). (For a gas grill, preheat grill. Reduce heat to medium-high. Adjust for indirect cooking. Place roast on a rack in a shallow roasting pan; place pan on grill rack over the burner that is turned off. Grill as directed.)

3 Remove meat from grill. Cover meat with foil; let stand for 15 minutes. Temperature of meat after standing should be 145°F.

PER SERVING 193 **CAL**; 10 g **FAT** (4 g **SAT**); 70 mg **CHOL**; 253 mg **SODIUM**; 2 g **CARB**; 0 g **FIBER**; 24 g **PRO**

STEAK REMOULADE SANDWICHES

Bison Burgers with Caramelized Dates and Onions

For those interested in heart-healthy eating (and who isn't?), bison belongs on the menu. Although buffalo meat tastes as rich and satisfying as beef, bison is extremely lean, lower in calories, and higher in iron content than beef.

MAKES 4 servings **PREP** 35 minutes **GRILL** 14 minutes

1	tablespoon Worcestershire sauce
2	cloves garlic, minced
¼	teaspoon black pepper
1	pound ground bison (buffalo)
2	medium sweet onions, halved and thinly sliced
6	cloves garlic, minced
2	tablespoons olive oil
½	cup chopped pitted dates
2	tablespoons dry red wine
4	slices sharp cheddar cheese (4 ounces)
4	slices sourdough bread or ciabatta bread or 8 large slices (½-inch-thick slices), toasted
1	cup arugula leaves

1 In a medium bowl combine Worcestershire sauce, the 2 cloves garlic, and pepper. Add ground bison; mix well. Shape meat mixture into four ¾-inch-thick oval patties. Set aside.

2 In a large skillet cook onions and the 6 cloves garlic in hot oil over medium heat about 10 minutes or until onions are tender and golden, stirring occasionally. Stir in dates and wine. Cook for 1 to 2 minutes more or until wine is nearly evaporated and mixture becomes syrupy. Remove from heat; cover and keep warm.

3 For a charcoal grill, grill patties on the rack of an uncovered grill directly over medium coals for 14 to 16 minutes or until done (160°F), turning once halfway through grilling. Add cheese to patties the last 2 minutes of grilling. (For a gas grill, preheat grill. Reduce heat to medium. Place patties on grill rack over heat. Cover; grill as directed.)

4 Serve patties between slices of bread with arugula and onion mixture.

PER SERVING 617 **CAL**; 25 g **FAT** (10 g **SAT**); 92 mg **CHOL**; 638 mg **SODIUM**; 60 g **CARB**; 4 g **FIBER**; 38 g **PRO**

Chicken-Apple Burgers

When selecting the meat for these yummy burgers, choose packages marked "ground chicken" or "ground turkey." These products contain leg and thigh meat in addition to breast, making them juicy and flavorful.

PREP 40 minutes **GRILL** 14 minutes

- **4**   slices bacon, chopped
- **½**   cup finely chopped onion (1 medium)
- **1**   tablespoon bottled minced garlic
- **½**   teaspoon black pepper
- **¼**   teaspoon salt
- **¼**   cup apple brandy, apple juice, or dry white wine
- **1**   medium Granny Smith apple, cored and finely chopped
- **2**   tablespoons snipped fresh parsley
- **1**   teaspoon snipped fresh sage
- **2**   pounds uncooked ground chicken or turkey
- **1**   cup soft bread crumbs
- **4**   1-ounce slices aged white cheddar cheese, Fontina cheese, or cheddar cheese
  Honey mustard
- **4**   whole wheat hamburger buns, split and toasted
  Butterhead (Bibb or Boston) lettuce leaves
  Thin slices Granny Smith apple (optional)

1 For apple filling, in a large skillet cook bacon over medium heat about 5 minutes or until browned and crisp. Transfer bacon to a paper towel-lined plate, reserving 1 teaspoon of the drippings in skillet. Add onion, garlic, pepper, and salt to reserved drippings in skillet; cook about 3 minutes or until onions are tender. Remove skillet from heat. Add apple brandy to hot skillet. Return to heat. Simmer, uncovered, until nearly all of the brandy has evaporated. Remove skillet from heat; stir in the cooked bacon, the chopped apple, parsley, and sage. Set aside to cool.

2 In a large bowl combine chicken and bread crumbs. Divide into eight portions. On a tray or baking sheet shape each portion into a 4-inch-diameter patty. Divide apple mixture among four of the patties. Top with the remaining four patties, pressing edges to seal well.

3 For a charcoal grill, grill patties on the rack of an uncovered grill directly over medium coals for 14 to 18 minutes or until done (165°F),* turning once halfway through grilling and topping with cheese the last 2 minutes of grilling. (For a gas grill, preheat grill. Reduce heat to medium. Place patties on grill rack over heat. Cover and grill as above.)

4 Spread the cut sides of bun halves with honey mustard. Serve patties in buns with lettuce and, if desired, apple slices.

*Note: The internal color of a patty is not a reliable doneness indicator. A chicken or turkey patty cooked to 165°F is safe, regardless of color. To measure the doneness of a patty, insert an instant-read thermometer through the side of the patty to a depth of 2 to 3 inches, making sure the tip of the thermometer is in the meat rather than in the apple filling.

PER SERVING 712 **CAL**; 32 g **FAT** (12 g **SAT**); 232 mg **CHOL**; 923 mg **SODIUM**; 43 g **CARB**; 4 g **FIBER**; 54 g **PRO**

SPICY BUFFALO CHICKEN SALAD

Grillers Stuffed with Spinach and Smoked Gouda

Taste how enticing an everyday chicken breast becomes when stuffed with this smoky, creamy mixture of mushrooms and cheese. Another time, prepare the stuffing and pocket it between two thin ground beef patties, making stuffed burgers!

MAKES 4 servings **PREP** 30 minutes **GRILL** 12 minutes

⅓	cup finely chopped onion (1 small)
2	cloves garlic, minced
1	tablespoon olive oil
1	cup chopped fresh mushrooms
1	cup shredded smoked Gouda cheese (4 ounces)
½	10-ounce package frozen chopped spinach, thawed and squeezed dry
¼	teaspoon ground nutmeg
4	skinless, boneless chicken breast halves

1 For filling, in a large skillet cook onion and garlic in hot oil over medium heat about 5 minutes or until onion is tender. Add mushrooms. Cook and stir about 5 minutes more or until mushrooms are tender. Remove from heat. Stir in cheese, spinach, and nutmeg. Set aside.

2 Using a sharp knife, cut a 2-inch pocket in the thickest part of each chicken breast half by cutting horizontally toward, but not through, the opposite side. Divide filling evenly among pockets in chicken. If necessary, secure openings with wooden toothpicks.

3 For a charcoal grill, grill chicken on the rack of an uncovered grill directly over medium coals for 12 to 15 minutes or until chicken is no longer pink (170°F), turning once halfway through grilling. (For a gas grill, preheat grill. Reduce heat to medium. Place chicken on grill rack over heat. Cover and grill as directed.) Remove and discard any toothpicks.

PER SERVING 328 **CAL**; 13 g **FAT** (6 g **SAT**); 121 mg **CHOL**; 578 mg **SODIUM**; 6 g **CARB**; 2 g **FIBER**; 47 g **PRO**

Spicy Buffalo Chicken Salad

By grilling lean, skinless, boneless chicken breasts and calling upon healthful, fiber-filled cabbage, carrots, and celery, the flavorful—but not so wholesome—Buffalo wings become a meal both delicious and nutritious.

MAKES 4 servings **PREP** 20 minutes **MARINATE** 3 hours **GRILL** 12 minutes

1	pound skinless, boneless chicken breast halves
2	tablespoons olive oil
1	tablespoon cider vinegar
1	tablespoon bottled hot pepper sauce or Louisiana hot sauce
⅓	cup bottled blue cheese salad dressing
½	teaspoon bottled hot pepper sauce or Louisiana hot sauce
2	cups shredded savoy or green cabbage
1	cup bite-size carrot strips (2 medium)
1	cup thinly sliced celery (2 stalks)
½	cup crumbled blue cheese (2 ounces)

1 Place chicken in a large resealable plastic bag set in a shallow dish. For marinade, in a small bowl stir together oil, vinegar, and the 1 tablespoon hot pepper sauce. Pour over chicken in bag; seal bag. Turn to coat chicken. Marinate in the refrigerator for 3 to 4 hours, turning bag occasionally.

2 Drain chicken, reserving marinade. For a charcoal grill, grill chicken on the rack of an uncovered grill directly over medium coals for 12 to 15 minutes or until chicken is no longer pink (170°F), turning and brushing once with reserved marinade halfway through grilling. (For a gas grill, preheat grill. Reduce heat to medium. Place chicken on grill rack over heat. Cover and grill as directed.) Discard any remaining marinade. Slice chicken diagonally.

3 In a medium serving bowl stir together blue cheese salad dressing and the ½ teaspoon hot pepper sauce. Add cabbage, carrots, celery, and three-fourths of the blue cheese. Toss to coat. Arrange sliced chicken on cabbage. Sprinkle with the remaining blue cheese.

PER SERVING 367 **CAL**; 23 g **FAT** (6 g **SAT**); 80 mg **CHOL**; 563 mg **SODIUM**; 8 g **CARB**; 3 g **FIBER**; 32 g **PRO**

Fish Sandwiches with Red Pepper-Onion Relish

American farmed catfish is one of the most sustainable fish species on the planet, making it a sound ecological choice—and one you can feel good about making.

MAKES 4 servings **PREP** 25 minutes **GRILL** 12 minutes

- **4** 4- to 5-ounce fresh or frozen skinless catfish or white-flesh fish fillets, ½ inch thick
- **1** tablespoon lemon juice or lime juice
- **1** teaspoon lemon-pepper seasoning, Jamaican jerk seasoning, or Cajun seasoning
- **1** large onion, quartered
- **1** large red sweet pepper, quartered
- **1** tablespoon olive oil
- **3** tablespoons snipped fresh parsley
- **2** tablespoons sugar
- **2** tablespoons cider vinegar
- **2** tablespoons balsamic vinegar
- **¼** teaspoon each salt and black pepper
- **4** round hard rolls, hoagie buns, kaiser rolls, or other crusty rolls, split and toasted

1 Thaw fish, if frozen. Rinse fish; pat dry with paper towels. Brush fish with lemon juice. Sprinkle seasoning evenly on all sides of fish. Set aside.

2 For the relish, brush onion and sweet pepper with oil. For a charcoal grill, grill onion and sweet pepper on the rack of an uncovered grill directly over medium coals for 8 to 10 minutes or until tender, turning occasionally. (For a gas grill, preheat grill. Reduce heat to medium. Place onion and sweet pepper on grill rack over heat. Cover and grill as directed.)

3 Transfer vegetables to a cutting board; cool until easy to handle. Chop vegetables and place in a bowl. Stir in parsley, sugar, vinegars, salt, and black pepper; toss to coat.

4 For a charcoal grill, grill fish on the greased rack of an uncovered grill directly over medium coals for 4 to 6 minutes or until fish begins to flake when tested with a fork, turning once halfway through grilling. (For a gas grill, preheat grill. Reduce heat to medium. Place fish on greased grill rack over heat. Cover and grill as directed.)

5 Serve fish on rolls. Using a slotted spoon, top with relish.

PER SERVING 473 **CAL**; 17 g **FAT** (3 g **SAT**); 53 mg **CHOL**; 892 mg **SODIUM**; 55 g **CARB**; 4 g **FIBER**; 25 g **PRO**

Salmon Caesar Salad

To prepare your grill rack quickly and easily for grilling delicate fish and seafood, just wad up a clean paper towel, dip in cooking oil, and holding the towel with tongs, rub it back and forth over the grill grates.

MAKES 4 servings **PREP** 25 minutes **GRILL** 8 minutes

- **1** pound fresh or frozen skinless salmon fillets, about 1 inch thick
- **1** tablespoon olive oil
- **1** teaspoon finely shredded lemon peel
- **1** tablespoon lemon juice
- **¼** teaspoon black pepper
- **1** pound fresh asparagus spears, trimmed
- **2** cups sliced hearts of romaine lettuce
- **2** cups torn curly endive
- **½** medium cucumber, thinly sliced
- **½** cup bottled Caesar salad dressing
    Finely shredded Parmesan cheese (optional)
    Thin slices baguette-style French bread, toasted (optional)

1 Thaw fish, if frozen. Rinse fish; pat dry with paper towels. In a small bowl stir together oil, lemon peel, lemon juice, and pepper. Brush both sides of fish with lemon mixture; set aside.

2 In a large skillet cook asparagus, covered, in a small amount of boiling water for 3 minutes; drain. Place asparagus in a grill wok.

3 For a charcoal grill, grill fish on the greased rack of an uncovered grill directly over medium coals for 8 to 12 minutes or until fish begins to flake when tested with a fork, turning once halfway through grilling. Add asparagus in wok to grill during the last 3 to 5 minutes of grilling or until asparagus browns, turning once halfway through grilling. (For a gas grill, preheat grill. Reduce heat to medium. Place fish, then asparagus in wok, on greased grill rack over heat. Cover and grill as directed.)

4 In a large bowl combine lettuce, endive, and cucumber. Divide evenly among serving plates. Using a fork, flake fish into bite-size pieces. Arrange fish and asparagus on greens. Drizzle salads with dressing. If desired, sprinkle with cheese and serve with toasted baguette slices.

PER SERVING 351 **CAL**; 25 g **FAT** (4 g **SAT**); 59 mg **CHOL**; 418 mg **SODIUM**; 5 g **CARB**; 3 g **FIBER**; 26 g **PRO**

FISH SANDWICHES WITH RED PEPPER-ONION RELISH

Shrimp Po' Boy with Dried Tomato Aïoli

There are countless explanations for the coinage of the word "Po' Boy," but perhaps the most credible is that the sandwiches were given to striking railroad workers—called "Poor Boys" by a sympathetic restaurateur.

MAKES 4 servings **PREP** 30 minutes **MARINATE** 1 hour **GRILL** 19 minutes

- **1** **pound fresh or frozen jumbo shrimp in shells**
- **2** **tablespoons lemon juice**
- **2** **tablespoons olive oil**
- **1** **teaspoon seafood seasoning (such as Old Bay)**
- **1** **8-ounce or ½ of a 16-ounce loaf unsliced French bread**
- **½** **cup mayonnaise**
- **¼** **cup chopped oil-packed dried tomatoes, drained**
- **2** **tablespoons sour cream**
- **2** **cloves garlic, minced**
- **½** **of a medium red onion, thinly sliced**
  Shredded lettuce (optional)

1 Thaw shrimp, if frozen. Peel and devein shrimp, removing tails. Rinse shrimp; pat dry with paper towels. Place shrimp in a large resealable plastic bag set in a shallow dish. For marinade, in a small bowl stir together 1 tablespoon of the lemon juice, 1 tablespoon of the olive oil, and the seafood seasoning. Pour over shrimp in bag; seal bag. Marinate in the refrigerator for 1 hour, turning bag occasionally. Thread shrimp on four long metal skewers, leaving ¼ inch between shrimp.

2 Cut bread in half horizontally. Use a spoon to hollow out the top half, leaving a ½-inch shell. Lightly brush cut sides of bread with remaining 1 tablespoon olive oil.

3 For a charcoal grill, grill shrimp on the rack of an uncovered grill directly over medium coals for 7 to 9 minutes or until shrimp are opaque, turning once halfway through grilling. Place bread, cut sides down, on grill rack over heat. Grill about 2 minutes or until lightly toasted. (For a gas grill, preheat grill. Reduce heat to medium. Place shrimp and bread on grill rack over heat. Cover and grill as directed.)

4 Meanwhile, in a small bowl stir together the remaining 1 tablespoon lemon juice, the mayonnaise, dried tomatoes, sour cream, and garlic. Spread on cut sides of toasted bread. Place bottom half of bread in the center of an 18-inch square of heavy-duty foil. Arrange shrimp and red onion slices on

top; add the top half of bread. Bring up two opposite edges of foil and seal with a double fold. Fold remaining edges together to completely enclose. Place packet on grill over heat; grill for 12 to 15 minutes or until heated through, turning once.

5 To serve, remove foil. from. If desired, remove top and add lettuce; replace top. Cut into four equal pieces.

PER SERVING 542 **CAL**; 34 g **FAT** (5 g **SAT**); 151 mg **CHOL**; 829 mg **SODIUM**; 34 g **CARB**; 2 g **FIBER**; 23 g **PRO**

Zucchini Crab Cakes

To ensure that your crabmeat is free of shell and cartilage, simply empty the container into a fine-mesh sieve and work through the meat with your fingers.

MAKES 4 servings **PREP** 20 minutes **GRILL** 8 minutes

- 1 cup coarsely shredded zucchini (1 medium)
- ¼ cup thinly sliced green onions (2)
- 2 teaspoons vegetable oil
- 1 egg, beaten
- ⅓ cup seasoned fine dry bread crumbs
- 1 tablespoon Dijon mustard
- 1 teaspoon snipped fresh thyme or ½ teaspoon dried thyme, crushed
- ⅛ to ¼ teaspoon cayenne pepper
- 6 ounces fresh lump crabmeat or one 6-ounce can crabmeat, drained, flaked, and cartilage removed (1 cup)
- 2 large red and/or yellow tomatoes, sliced ¼ inch thick
- 1 recipe Tomato Sour Cream Sauce
  Lemon and/or lime wedges (optional)

1 In a medium skillet cook zucchini and green onions in hot oil over medium-high heat for 3 to 5 minutes or just until tender and liquid is evaporated. Cool slightly.

2 In a large bowl combine egg, bread crumbs, mustard, thyme, and cayenne pepper. Add crabmeat and the zucchini mixture; mix well. Using about ¼ cup per crab cake, shape mixture into eight ½-inch-thick patties.

3 For a charcoal grill, grill crab cakes on the greased rack of an uncovered grill directly over medium coals for 8 to 10 minutes or until golden, turning once halfway through grilling. (For a gas grill, preheat grill. Reduce heat to medium. Place crab cakes on greased grill rack over heat. Cover and grill as directed.)

4 To serve, arrange tomato slices and crab cakes on plates. Serve with Tomato-Sour Cream Sauce and, if desired, lemon wedges.

Tomato Sour Cream Sauce: In a small bowl stir together ½ cup sour cream, ¼ cup finely chopped, seeded yellow or red tomato, 1 tablespoon lemon juice, and ⅛ teaspoon seasoned salt. Cover and chill until serving time.

PER SERVING 243 **CAL**; 10 g **FAT** (4 g **SAT**); 120 mg **CHOL**; 835 mg **SODIUM**; 20 g **CARB**; 1 g **FIBER**; 18 g **PRO**

CHAPTER 6

healthy favorites

Recipes that combine healthy ingredients and heavenly flavors.

ROASTED VEGETABLE PITAS

Sauteed Pork Chops with Apples

Feel free to choose any tart—or baking—apple when preparing this fantastic fall dish. For added complexity, combine apple varieties at will.

MAKES 4 servings **PREP** 20 minutes **CHILL** 1 hour **COOK** 18 minutes

- **4   8-ounce bone-in pork center-cut chops, cut ¾ inch thick**
- **2   teaspoons canola oil**
- **1   tablespoon Sugar and Spice Rub**
- **1   tablespoon canola oil**
- **¼   cup dry white wine**
- **2   cups thinly sliced Granny Smith apples**
- **½   cup reduced-sodium chicken broth or chicken stock**
- **Fresh thyme sprigs**

1 Trim fat from chops. Brush the 2 teaspoons oil over all sides of chops. Sprinkle chops evenly with Sugar and Spice Rub; rub in with your fingers. Cover with plastic wrap; chill in refrigerator for 1 hour.

2 Preheat a large skillet over medium-high heat for 2 minutes. Add the 1 tablespoon oil; swirl to lightly coat skillet. Add chops; cook for 7 to 8 minutes or until golden brown and juices run clear (145°F), turning once. Transfer chops to a warm platter; cover and keep warm.

3 Remove skillet from heat. Slowly add wine to hot skillet, stirring to scrape up any browned bits from bottom of skillet. Return skillet to heat. Add sliced apples, broth, and 1 sprig of thyme. Bring to boiling; reduce heat. Simmer, covered, about 3 minutes or just until apples are tender. Using a slotted spoon, transfer apples to a small bowl; cover and keep warm. Bring broth mixture in skillet to boiling. Boil about 5 minutes or until liquid is reduced by half. Return chops and apples to skillet; heat through. Garnish with additional sprigs of fresh thyme and serve immediately.

Sugar and Spice Rub: In a small bowl stir together 2 tablespoons packed brown sugar, 2 teaspoons chili powder, 1½ teaspoons kosher salt, 1½ teaspoons garlic powder, 1½ teaspoons onion powder, 1½ teaspoons ground cumin, ¾ teaspoon cayenne pepper, and ¾ teaspoon black pepper. Store in an airtight container for up to 3 months. Makes about ½ cup.

PER SERVING 297 **CAL**; 12 g **FAT** (2 g **SAT**); 108 mg **CHOL**; 256 mg **SODIUM**; 9 g **CARB**; 2 g **FIBER**; 35 g **PRO**

Sweet-and-Sour Pork

Two simple, truly undetectable changes—substituting reduced-sodium chicken broth and reduced-sodium soy sauce for their regular, super salty counterparts—makes this recipe more healthful than it's ever been.

MAKES 6 servings **START TO FINISH** 30 minutes

- ¾ **cup reduced-sodium chicken broth**
- 3 **tablespoons red wine vinegar**
- 2 **tablespoons reduced-sodium soy sauce**
- 4 **teaspoons sugar**
- 1 **tablespoon cornstarch**
- 1 **garlic, minced**
- 4 **teaspoons cooking oil**
- 2 **medium carrots, thinly sliced (1 cup)**
- 1 **medium red sweet pepper, cut into bite-size strips (1 cup)**
- 1 **cup fresh pea pods, trimmed**
- 12 **ounces boneless pork loin, trimmed of fat and cut into 1-inch pieces**
- 1 **8-ounce can pineapple chunks (juice pack), drained**
- 3 **cups hot cooked brown rice**

1 For sauce, in a small bowl stir together broth, vinegar, soy sauce, sugar, cornstarch, and garlic; set aside.

2 In a large nonstick skillet heat 3 teaspoons of the oil over medium-high heat. Add carrots and sweet pepper; cook and stir for 3 minutes. Add pea pods. Cook and stir about 1 minute more or until vegetables are crisp-tender. Remove from skillet; set aside.

3 Add remaining 1 teaspoon oil to skillet. Add pork to skillet. Cook and stir for 4 to 6 minutes or until pork is slightly pink in the center. Push pork from center of skillet. Stir sauce; add to center of skillet. Cook and stir until thickened and bubbly. Add vegetables and pineapple chunks; heat through. Serve over hot cooked rice.

PER SERVING 288 **CAL**; 8 g **FAT** (2 g **SAT**); 31 mg **CHOL**; 310 mg **SODIUM**; 37 g **CARB**; 3 g **FIBER**; 16 g **PRO**

Vegetable-Mango Beef Stir-Fry

Amateur home cook Sheryl Little of Sherwood, Arkansas, wowed judges at the 29th Annual National Beef Cook-Off with the unique flavors and nutritional benefits of her Vegetable-Mango Beef Stir-Fry. Her Grand Prize, awarded at the Metropolitan Cooking and Entertaining Show in Washington, D.C., netted the avid recipe contest contestant—who uses friends and neighbors as her taste testers—$25,000, which she used to purchase new kitchen cabinets.

MAKES 4 servings **PREP** 15 minutes **COOK** 9 minutes

1 **pound boneless beef top sirloin steak, cut 1 inch thick**

1 **tablespoon extra virgin olive oil**

2 **cups jicama strips (1½ x ¼ inch)**

1 **8-ounce package fresh sugar snap pea pods (about 3 cups)**

1 **red sweet pepper, cut into thin strips**

1 **cup fresh mango chunks**

⅓ **cup low-sodium soy sauce**

3 **cloves garlic, minced**

3 **cups instant hot cooked rice**

1 If desired, partially freeze beef for easy slicing. Trim fat from meat. Thinly slice meat across the grain into bite-size strips; set aside.

2 In a large nonstick skillet heat 1 teaspoon of the oil over medium-high heat. Add half the beef; cook and stir 1 to 2 minutes. Remove from skillet. Repeat with 1 teaspoon oil and remaining beef. Remove from skillet and keep beef warm.

3 Heat remaining 1 teaspoon oil in the same skillet over medium-high heat. Add jicama; cook and stir 1 minute. Add sugar snap peas and sweet bell pepper; cook and stir 4 minutes or until vegetables are crisp-tender.

4 Return beef to skillet. Carefully stir in mango, soy sauce, and garlic. Cook for 2 minutes or until heated through. Serve over rice.

PER SERVING 509 **CAL**; 19 g **FAT** (6 g **SAT**); 85 mg **CHOL**; 833 mg **SODIUM**; 53 g **CARB**; 6 g **FIBER**; 30 g **PRO**

Southern Beefy Skillet

This family-friendly concoction, often called Calico Beans on the church supper and potluck circuits, brings 30 grams of inexpensive protein to the table in 40 minutes.

MAKES 4 servings **START TO FINISH** 40 minutes

1	**pound lean ground beef**
1	**cup chopped celery (2 stalks)**
½	**cup chopped onion (1 medium)**
2	**cloves garlic, minced**
1	**15.5- to 16-ounce can butter beans, rinsed and drained**
1	**14.5-ounce can no-salt-added diced tomatoes, undrained**
1	**8-ounce can no-salt-added tomato sauce**
1	**medium green sweet pepper, cut into bite-size strips (1 cup)**
1	**jalapeño, seeded and finely chopped (see note, page 15)**
2	**teaspoons Worcestershire sauce**
1	**teaspoon dried basil, crushed**
1	**teaspoon dried oregano, crushed**
½	**teaspoon bottled hot pepper sauce**
¼	**teaspoon black pepper**

1 In a large skillet cook ground beef, celery, onion, and garlic over medium heat until meat is browned, stirring to break up meat as it cooks. Drain off fat.

2 Add butter beans, tomatoes, tomato sauce, sweet pepper, jalapeño, Worcestershire sauce, basil, oregano, hot pepper sauce, and black pepper. Bring to boiling; reduce heat. Simmer, uncovered, for 10 to 15 minutes or until desired consistency.

PER SERVING 342 **CAL**; 12 g **FAT** (5 g **SAT**); 74 mg **CHOL**; 499 mg **SODIUM**; 33 g **CARB**; 9 g **FIBER**; 30 g **PRO**

Smashed Potato Chicken Pot Pie

If your family is fond of Shepherd's Pie, they will clamor for this dish made with a creamy chicken and vegetable mixture.

MAKES 6 servings **PREP** 25 minutes **BAKE** 30 minutes at 375°F **STAND** 5 minutes

- **3 tablespoons butter or margarine**
- **⅓ cup all-purpose flour**
- **1 teaspoon seasoned pepper**
- **¼ teaspoon salt**
- **1 14.5-ounce can reduced-sodium chicken broth**
- **¾ cup milk**
- **2½ cups chopped chicken or turkey**
- **2 cups frozen peas and carrots, thawed**
- **2 cups frozen cut green beans, thawed**
- **1 24-ounce package refrigerated mashed potatoes**
- **2 tablespoons grated Parmesan cheese**
- **1 clove garlic, minced**

1 Preheat oven to 375°F. In a large saucepan melt butter over medium heat. Stir in flour, ½ teaspoon of the seasoned pepper, and the salt. Add broth and milk all at once. Cook and stir until thickened and bubbly. Stir in cooked chicken and thawed vegetables. Pour into a 3-quart baking dish.

2 In a medium bowl combine mashed potatoes, Parmesan cheese, garlic, and the remaining ½ teaspoon seasoned pepper. Using a spoon, drop potato mixture in large mounds over chicken mixture in baking dish.

3 Bake, uncovered, for 30 to 40 minutes or until heated through. Let stand for 5 minutes before serving.

PER SERVING 330 **CAL**; 13 g **FAT** (6 g **SAT**); 72 mg **CHOL**; 616 mg **SODIUM**; 29 g **CARB**; 4 g **FIBER**; 25 g **PRO**

Tropical Chicken Salad Wraps

Napa cabbage—also called Chinese cabbage—has pale green, crinkly leaves that are thinner, crisper, and milder than those of standard cabbage.

MAKES 4 servings **START TO FINISH** 25 minutes

- **2 cups shredded cooked chicken breast**
- **2 cups finely shredded napa cabbage**
- **1 8-ounce can crushed pineapple, drained**
- **⅓ cup light mayonnaise**
- **2 tablespoons flaked coconut, toasted**
- **1 tablespoon lime juice**
- **1 tablespoon chopped fresh cilantro**
- **1 teaspoon Jamaican jerk seasoning**
- **8 leaves Bibb or Boston lettuce**
   Lime wedges (optional)

1 In a large bowl combine chicken, shredded cabbage, drained pineapple, mayonnaise, coconut, lime juice, cilantro, and Jamaican jerk seasoning.

2 Divide chicken salad among leaves. If desired, serve with lime wedges.

PER SERVING 243 **CAL**; 10 g **FAT** (3 g **SAT**); 66 mg **CHOL**; 301 mg **SODIUM**; 14 g **CARB**; 1 g **FIBER**; 23 g **PRO**

Chicken, Macaroni, and Cheese

With the use of reduced-fat cheeses and the addition of juicy tomatoes and tender spinach, this creamy, stove-top macaroni and cheese will fool even the pickiest palates into thinking it's the full-fat version.

MAKES 5 servings **START TO FINISH** 35 minutes

1½ **cups dried multigrain or regular elbow macaroni (6 ounces)**
   Nonstick cooking spray
12 **ounces skinless, boneless chicken breast halves, cut into 1-inch pieces**
¼ **cup finely chopped onion**
1   **6.5-ounce package light semisoft cheese with garlic and herb**
1⅔ **cups fat-free milk**
1   **tablespoon flour**
¾ **cup shredded reduced-fat cheddar cheese (3 ounces)**
2   **cups packaged fresh baby spinach**
1   **cup chopped, seeded tomatoes**

1 In a medium saucepan cook macaroni according to package directions, except do not add salt to the water; drain.

2 Meanwhile, coat a large unheated nonstick skillet with cooking spray; heat skillet over medium-high heat. Add chicken and onion to skillet. Cook for 4 to 6 minutes or until chicken is no longer pink and onion is tender, stirring frequently. If onion browns too quickly, reduce heat to medium. Remove skillet from heat. Stir in semisoft cheese until melted.

3 In a medium bowl whisk together milk and flour until smooth. Add all at once to chicken mixture. Cook and stir over medium heat until thickened and bubbly. Reduce heat to low. Stir in cheddar cheese until melted. Add cooked macaroni; cook and stir for 1 to 2 minutes or until heated through. Stir in spinach and tomatoes. Serve immediately.

PER SERVING 369 **CAL**; 12 g **FAT** (7 g **SAT**); 85 mg **CHOL**; 393 mg **SODIUM**; 33 g **CARB**; 4 g **FIBER**; 33 g **PRO**

FRESH BRUSCHETTA CHICKEN-
STUFFED TOMATOES

Fresh Bruschetta Chicken-Stuffed Tomatoes

Deli-roasted chicken holds the key to the lock on fabulous, fuss-free meals, and this scrumptious, Italian-inspired recipe proves it.

MAKES 4 servings   **START TO FINISH** 25 minutes

1	**2- to 2½ pound deli-roasted chicken**
1	**cup fresh spinach leaves, coarsely chopped**
¼	**cup thinly sliced green onions (2)**
¼	**cup snipped fresh basil or 2 teaspoons dried basil, crushed**
2	**tablespoons white balsamic vinegar or regular balsamic vinegar**
1	**tablespoon olive oil**
2	**cloves garlic, minced**
4	**large tomatoes (8 to 10 ounces each)**
2	**very thin slices firm-texture whole wheat bread, toasted and cut into cubes**
2	**tablespoons shredded Parmesan cheese**

1 Remove and discard skin from chicken. Cut meat off the bones. Chop enough meat to measure 2 cups; save the remaining chicken for another use. In a medium bowl combine the 2 cups chicken, the spinach, green onions, basil, vinegar, oil, and garlic. Toss to evenly coat.

2 Cut a ¼-inch slice from the stem end of each tomato; discard slices. Using a spoon, carefully scoop out tomato pulp, leaving a ¼- to ½-inch shell. Place shells, open sides up, on serving plate. Discard tomato seeds. Chop enough of the tomato pulp to measure ½ cup; discard remaining pulp. Stir the ½ cup tomato pulp into chicken filling.

3 Divide chicken filling among tomato shells. Top with bread cubes and cheese.

PER SERVING 249 **CAL**; 14 g **FAT** (4 g **SAT**); 64 mg **CHOL**; 509 mg **SODIUM**; 16 g **CARB**; 4 g **FIBER**; 17 g **PRO**

Salmon and Couscous Casserole

With every ingredient a pantry or refrigerator staple, this is the kind of recipe that you can throw together in minutes, creating a healthful family meal on those busy, after-work weeknights.

MAKES 4 servings **START TO FINISH** 25 minutes

1	**cup water**
2	**cloves garlic, minced**
⅔	**cup whole wheat couscous**
1	**14.75-ounce can salmon, drained, flaked, and skin and bones removed**
2	**cups packaged fresh baby spinach leaves**
½	**cup jarred roasted red sweet peppers, drained and chopped**
⅓	**cup jarred tomato bruschetta topper**
2	**tablespoons purchased toasted almonds**
1	**lemon, quartered (optional)**

1 In a 2-quart microwave-safe casserole combine the water and garlic. Heat, uncovered, on high for 2½ to 3 minutes or until boiling. Remove from microwave and stir in couscous. Spoon salmon on couscous. Cover; let stand for 5 minutes.

2 Add spinach, roasted peppers, and bruschetta topper to couscous. Toss to combine. Divide among four serving plates. Top with almonds. If desired, squeeze with lemon.

PER SERVING 335 **CAL**; 9 g **FAT** (2 g **SAT**); 41 mg **CHOL**; 616 mg **SODIUM**; 34 g **CARB**; 6 g **FIBER**; 30 g **PRO**

Tuscan Tuna with Tomato Salad

Mark this recipe for late summer, when flavorful, garden-grown tomatoes make their juicy debut. With heirloom tomato varieties, you can concoct this salad with red, yellow, orange—or even white, brown, or purple—tomatoes.

MAKES 4 servings   **PREP** 15 minutes   **GRILL** 6 minutes

4	5- to 6-ounce fresh or frozen tuna steaks, about 1 inch thick
3	teaspoons white wine vinegar
1	teaspoon olive oil
½	teaspoon dried Italian seasoning, crushed
¼	teaspoon salt
¼	teaspoon black pepper
1	cup seeded and chopped tomatoes (2 medium)
½	cup thinly sliced fennel bulb
¼	cup snipped fresh basil
1	medium shallot, halved and thinly sliced
1	clove garlic, minced
¼	teaspoon black pepper
1	tablespoon pine nuts, toasted and chopped*
1	tablespoon finely shredded Parmesan cheese

1 Thaw fish, if frozen. Rinse fish; pat dry with paper towels. Set aside. In a small bowl stir together 1 teaspoon of the vinegar, the olive oil, Italian seasoning, salt, and ¼ teaspoon pepper. Brush on both sides of tuna steaks. Set aside.

2 For tomato salad, in a medium bowl stir together tomatoes, fennel, basil, shallot, garlic, the remaining 2 teaspoons vinegar, and ¼ teaspoon pepper. Set aside.

3 For a charcoal grill, place fish on the greased grill rack directly over medium coals. Grill, uncovered, for 6 to 8 minutes or until fish begins to flake when tested with a fork, turning fish once halfway through grilling. (For a gas grill, preheat grill. Reduce heat to medium. Place fish on a greased grill rack over heat. Cover and grill as directed.)

4 Serve tuna with tomato salad. Sprinkle with pine nuts and Parmesan cheese.

*Note: Toast pine nuts in a dry skillet over medium heat, shaking the skillet frequently to prevent burning.

PER SERVING 255 **CAL**; 10 g **FAT** (2 g **SAT**); 55 mg **CHOL**; 232 mg **SODIUM**; 5 g **CARB**; 1 g **FIBER**; 35 g **PRO**

FISH AND CHIPS-STYLE COD

Fish and Chips-Style Cod

The most important step in this recipe is patting the fish dry with paper towels. Drying fish will allow the batter to adhere to the flesh and make the strips turn out nice and crispy.

MAKES 4 servings **PREP** 20 minutes **CHILL** 30 minutes
COOK 4 minutes per batch

1 **pound fresh or frozen cod or halibut fillets**
½ **cup flour**
⅓ **cup fat-free milk**
⅓ **cup ale or nonalcoholic beer**
1 **egg or ¼ cup refrigerated or frozen egg product, thawed**
¼ **teaspoon kosher salt**
  Freshly ground black pepper
½ **cup canola oil**
  Malt vinegar
1 **recipe Fried Parsley (optional)**

1 Thaw fish, if frozen. Set aside. For batter, in a medium bowl whisk together flour, milk, ale, egg, salt, and pepper until combined. Cover and chill batter for 30 minutes.

2 Preheat oven to 250°F. Rinse fish under cold running water; pat dry with paper towels. Cut fish crosswise into eight pieces total.

3 In an medium skillet heat oil over medium-high heat for minutes. Dip four pieces of the fish in the batter, turning to coat and letting excess batter drip off. Fry the fish pieces in the hot oil about 4 minutes or until golden brown and fish flakes easily when tested with a fork, turning once. Transfer fried fish to paper towels; let stand to drain. Place fish on a baking sheet; keep warm in the oven. Repeat with remaining fish pieces.

4 Serve fish with malt vinegar and, if desired, garnish with Fried Parsley.

PER SERVING 177 **CAL**; 8 g **FAT** (1 g **SAT**); 55 mg **CHOL**; 118 mg **SODIUM**; 4 g **CARB**; 0 g **FIBER**; 21 g **PRO**

Fried Parsley: After cooking fish in the oil, add several sprigs of fresh parsley to the hot oil. Cook until parsley is no longer bubbly. Using a slotted spoon, remove parsley from oil. Drain on paper towels.

Asian Sesame Noodles with Shrimp

Big appetites and low calorie counts do not often get along, but they sure do here. This fresh, full-flavor Asian-style mixture contains only 285 calories in a generous 1¼-cup portion.

MAKES 4 servings **START TO FINISH** 30 minutes

8 **ounces fresh or frozen shrimp, peeled and deveined**
6 **ounces udon noodles**
1 **cup snow peas, trimmed and halved diagonally**
⅔ **cup carrots, julienned**
½ **cup bok choy, thinly sliced**
2 **tablespoons rice vinegar**
1 **tablespoon canola oil**
2 **teaspoons grated fresh ginger**
1 **teaspoon reduced-sodium soy sauce**
1 **teaspoon toasted sesame oil**
1 **clove garlic, minced**
½ **teaspoon honey**
¼ **teaspoon crushed red pepper**
⅛ **teaspoon salt**
1 **teaspoon sesame seeds, toasted**

1 Thaw shrimp, if frozen. Cook noodles according to package directions, adding shrimp and snow peas during the last 3 minutes of cooking time; drain. Rinse under cold running water to stop cooking; drain again.

2 In a serving bowl combine noodle mixture, carrots, and bok choy. For dressing, in a screw-top jar combine rice vinegar, canola oil, ginger, soy sauce, sesame oil, garlic, honey, crushed red pepper, and salt. Pour dressing over noodle mixture and toss to coat. Sprinkle with sesame seeds. Cover and chill until ready to serve or up to 2 hours.

PER SERVING 285 **CAL**; 7 g **FAT** (1 g **SAT**); 86 mg **CHOL**; 284 mg **SODIUM**; 35 g **CARB**; 4 g **FIBER**; 19 g **PRO**

Spicy Vegetable Fried Rice

Fried rice—normally a fat- and calorie-laden dish—is reinvented and "healthified" right here by simply using nonstick spray instead of oil and a nonstick skillet that makes the brown rice and veggie-packed mixture easy to stir.

MAKES 4 servings **START TO FINISH** 30 minutes

4	**eggs**
2	**tablespoons water**
	Nonstick cooking spray
1	**tablespoon finely chopped, peeled fresh ginger**
2	**cloves garlic, minced**
1	**tablespoon olive oil**
2	**cups chopped napa cabbage**
1	**cup coarsely shredded carrots (2 medium)**
1	**cup fresh pea pods, trimmed**
2	**cups cooked brown rice**
⅓	**cup sliced green onions**
2	**tablespoons reduced-sodium soy sauce**
1	**to 2 teaspoons Sriracha chile sauce**
2	**tablespoons snipped fresh cilantro**
	Lime slices or wedges

1 In a small bowl whisk together eggs and the water. Coat a large unheated nonstick skillet with cooking spray. Preheat skillet over medium heat. Pour in egg mixture. Cook, without stirring, until eggs begin to set on the bottom and around the edges. With a spatula or large spoon, lift and fold the partially cooked eggs so the uncooked portion flows underneath. Continue cooking over medium heat for 2 to 3 minutes or until cooked through but still glossy and moist, keeping eggs in large pieces. Carefully transfer eggs to a medium bowl; set aside.

2 In the same skillet cook and stir ginger and garlic in hot oil over medium-high heat for 30 seconds. Add cabbage, carrots, and pea pods; cook and stir for 2 minutes. Stir in cooked eggs, brown rice, green onions, soy sauce, and chile sauce; cook and stir about 2 minutes or until heated through. Top with cilantro. Serve with lime slices.

PER SERVING 250 **CAL**; 9 g **FAT** (2 g **SAT**); 212 mg **CHOL**; 367 mg **SODIUM**; 31 g **CARB**; 4 g **FIBER**; 11 g **PRO**

Roasted Vegetable Pitas

Pile the caramelized goodness of roasted eggplant, zucchini, peppers, onions, and tomatoes into whole grain pitas to create a vegetarian delight perfect for Meatless Mondays.

MAKES 4 servings **PREP** 25 minutes **ROAST** 25 minutes at 400°F

- **1½ cups coarsely chopped Japanese eggplant (1 small)**
- **1¼ cups coarsely chopped zucchini (1 small)**
- **1¼ cups coarsely chopped red or yellow sweet pepper (1 large)**
- **1 cup coarsely chopped red onion (1 small)**
- **4 cloves garlic, sliced**
- **2 tablespoons olive oil**
- **1 teaspoon dried oregano, crushed**
- **¼ teaspoon crushed red pepper**
- **¼ teaspoon salt**
- **1 cup yellow pear or cherry tomatoes, halved**
- **1 tablespoon lemon juice**
- **2 whole wheat pita bread rounds, halved**
- **¼ cup plain Greek fat-free yogurt**
- **¼ cup crumbled reduced-fat feta cheese**

1 Preheat oven to 400°F. In a large bowl combine eggplant, zucchini, sweet pepper, onion, garlic, olive oil, oregano, crushed red pepper, and salt. Toss to combine. Spread vegetables in a shallow roasting pan. Roast, uncovered, for 15 minutes. Add tomatoes; stir until combined. Roast about 10 minutes more or until vegetables are lightly browned and tender.

2 Drizzle vegetables with lemon juice; toss to coat. Divide vegetables among four pita bread halves. Top with yogurt and sprinkle with feta. Serve immediately.

PER SERVING 225 **CAL**; 9 g **FAT** (2 g **SAT**); 3 mg **CHOL**; 448 mg **SODIUM**; 31 g **CARB**; 6 g **FIBER**; 8 g **PRO**

potluck
pleasers

Crowd-friendly recipes expressly meant for sharing.

BEEF STROGANOFF CASSEROLE

BEEF

Beef Stroganoff Casserole, 133

Reuben Sandwich Casserole, 132

CHICKEN

French Cassoulet with Lentils, Bacon, Sausage,
and Chicken Confit, 131

MEATLESS

Cheese Fondue Casserole, 135

Creamy Artichoke Lasagna Bake, 135

Italian Pinhead Torta, 137

SOUPS

Chicken and Sausage Gumbo, 138

Three-Cheese Beer Soup, 138

SIDE DISHES

Chile-Cheddar Casserole Bread, 143

Creamy Hot Chicken Salad, 147

Five-Herb Roasted Carrots and Potatoes, 140

Herbed Yukon Gold and Sweet Potato Gratin, 141

Home-Style Green Bean Bake, 142

Layered California-Style BLT Salad, 145

Mediterranean Wild Rice Salad, 146

Spicy Apricot and Sausage Braid, 144

French Cassoulet with Lentils, Bacon, Sausage, and Chicken Confit

Retired journalist-turned-novelist Lily Julow of Gainesville, Florida, began developing recipes when living in Nice, France, in the '70s. Immersed in a culture in which "buying and preparing food is viewed as a major art form and every dish, even the simplest, is startling in its perfection" gave her insight into preparing simple, classic dishes with organic foods such as lentils. Judges at the 2012 Legendary Lentil Festival in Pullman, Washington, raved over her cassoulet, awarding it their top prize along with $1,000.

MAKES 6 to 8 servings **PREP** 30 minutes **STAND** 2 hours **CHILL** 12 hours **COOK** 45 minutes **BAKE** 30 minutes at 350°F

1	**pound dried lentils**
5	**tablespoons extra virgin olive oil**
4	**ounces coarsely chopped pancetta (½-inch pieces)**
½	**cup coarsely chopped onion (1 medium)**
4	**thyme sprigs**
4	**cups chicken broth**
3	**cups water**
1	**large bulb garlic, cloves peeled (10 to 12 cloves)**
1	**purchased roasted chicken, skin removed if desired and cut into 8 pieces**
8	**ounces coarsely chopped salami (½-inch-thick pieces)**
4	**ounces lean slab bacon, cut into 1-inch cubes**
2	**cups coarse fresh white bread crumbs**
2	**tablespoons chopped fresh parsley**

1 Soak lentils in enough water to cover for 2 hours; drain. In a large pot heat 3 tablespoons of the olive oil over medium heat; add pancetta and cook and stir for 3 to 5 minutes or until fat is rendered. Add onion; cook and stir 4 minutes or until tender. Add lentils, thyme, broth, and 2 cups of the water; bring to boiling. Reduce heat and simmer, covered, 30 minutes, stirring occasionally. Add garlic; cover and simmer about 15 minutes more or until garlic and lentils are tender, stirring occasionally. Remove and discard thyme sprigs. Cool mixture slightly. Transfer to a large bowl or container; cover and chill overnight.

2 Preheat oven to 350°F. Transfer the lentil mixture to the large pot. Stir in remaining 1 cup water. Heat over medium heat until simmering, stirring occasionally. Transfer to a 3-quart rectangular baking dish; arrange chicken pieces, salami, and bacon on the lentil mixture, pressing in slightly. Bake, uncovered, for 30 minutes or until bubbly and heated through. Remove from oven; set aside.

3 In a medium skillet heat remaining 2 tablespoons oil; add bread crumbs and cook over medium-high heat, stirring constantly, for 3 to 5 minutes or until browned and crisp. Sprinkle bread crumbs and parsley over cassoulet.

PER SERVING 956 **CAL**; 54 g **FAT** (15 g **SAT**); 185 mg **CHOL**; 2,292 mg **SODIUM**; 57 g **CARB**; 24 g **FIBER**; 63 g **PRO**

Reuben Sandwich Casserole

There's really nothing quite like this ingenious casserole—it's really a creamy Reuben sandwich that you eat with a fork.

MAKES 8 to 10 servings   **PREP** 20 minutes   **BAKE** 40 minutes at 375°F

- 1 **32-ounce jar sauerkraut, rinsed and drained**
- ½ **cup chopped onion (1 medium)**
- 4 **teaspoons dried parsley flakes, crushed**
- 2 **teaspoons caraway seeds**
- 4 **cups shredded Swiss cheese (1 pound)**
- 1⅓ **cups Thousand Island salad dressing**
- 12 **ounces thinly sliced cooked corned beef, coarsely chopped**
- 12 **slices party (pumpernickel or rye) bread**
- ¼ **cup butter, melted**

1 Preheat oven to 375°F. In a large bowl stir together drained sauerkraut, onion, parsley, and caraway seeds. Transfer sauerkraut mixture to a 3-quart rectangular baking dish. Top evenly with 1½ cups of the cheese, ⅔ cup of the salad dressing, and all of the corned beef. Top with the remaining ⅔ cup salad dressing and 1½ cups of the cheese.

2 Brush bread slices with melted butter. Arrange on top of casserole.

3 Bake, uncovered, about 35 minutes or until heated through and bread is toasted. Top with remaining cheese; bake about 5 minutes more or until cheese is melted.

PER SERVING 596 **CAL**; 45 g **FAT** (18 g **SAT**); 120 mg **CHOL**; 3,872 mg **SODIUM**; 22 g **CARB**; 10 g **FIBER**; 26 g **PRO**

Beef Stroganoff Casserole

This recipe takes advantage of today's time-saving, refrigerated cooked meat products such as this recipe's beef roast au jus. You'll find it's moist, succulent, and tasty too.

MAKES 6 servings **PREP** 35 minutes **BAKE** 30 minutes at 350°F

12	ounces dried campanelle or penne pasta
1	17-ounce package refrigerated cooked beef roast au jus
2	large fresh portobello mushrooms
2	tablespoons butter
1	medium sweet onion, cut into thin wedges
2	cloves garlic, minced
3	tablespoons all-purpose flour
2	tablespoons tomato paste
1	14.5-ounce can beef broth
1	tablespoon Worcestershire sauce
1	teaspoon smoked paprika or Spanish paprika
¼	teaspoon salt
¼	teaspoon black pepper
	Snipped fresh parsley (optional)
½	cup sour cream
1	tablespoon prepared horseradish
1	teaspoon snipped fresh dill or ¼ teaspoon dried dill

1 Preheat oven to 350°F. Cook pasta according to package directions; drain. Meanwhile, place roast on a cutting board; reserve juices. Using two forks, pull meat apart into bite-size pieces; set aside.

2 Remove and discard stems and gills from mushrooms; coarsely chop mushroom caps (you should have about 4 cups). In a large skillet heat butter over medium heat until melted. Add mushrooms, onion, and garlic; cook for 4 to 5 minutes or until onion is tender, stirring occasionally. Stir in flour and tomato paste. Add broth, Worcestershire sauce, paprika, salt, pepper, and the reserved meat juices. Cook and stir until thickened and bubbly. Remove from heat. Stir in pasta and meat.

3 Transfer mixture to an ungreased 3-quart casserole or rectangular baking dish. Bake, covered, about 30 minutes or until heated through. If desired, sprinkle with parsley.

4 Meanwhile, in a small bowl combine sour cream, horseradish, and dill. Spoon sour cream mixture over each serving.

PER SERVING 450 **CAL**; 14 g **FAT** (7 g **SAT**); 61 mg **CHOL**; 994 mg **SODIUM**; 57 g **CARB**; 4 g **FIBER**; 26 g **PRO**

CREAMY ARTICHOKE LASAGNA BAKE

Creamy Artichoke Lasagna Bake

MAKES 12 servings **PREP** 50 minutes
BAKE 35 minutes at 350°F **STAND** 15 minutes

 9 dried lasagna noodles
 3 tablespoons olive oil
 2 9-ounce packages frozen artichoke hearts, thawed and halved lengthwise
 ½ cup pine nuts
 4 cloves garlic, minced
 1 15-ounce carton ricotta cheese
 1 cup finely shredded Parmesan cheese (4 ounces)
 1 cup snipped fresh basil
 1 egg
 1 cup chicken broth or vegetable broth
 ¼ cup all-purpose flour
 2 cups half-and-half or light cream
 1 cup shredded mozzarella cheese (4 ounces)

1 Preheat oven to 350°F. Cook lasagna noodles according to package directions. Place lasagna noodles in a single layer on a sheet of foil; set aside.

2 In a saucepan heat 2 tablespoons of the oil over medium heat. Add artichokes, pine nuts, and half of the garlic. Cook for 2 to 3 minutes or until artichokes are tender. Transfer to a bowl. Stir in ricotta cheese, ½ cup of the Parmesan cheese, ½ cup of the basil, egg, and ¾ teaspoon salt.

3 For sauce, in a bowl combine broth and flour. In the same saucepan cook and stir remaining garlic in remaining 1 tablespoon oil over medium heat for 30 seconds. Stir in flour mixture and half-and-half. Cook and stir until thickened and bubbly. Remove from heat. Stir in the remaining ½ cup basil.

4 In a bowl combine mozzarella cheese and the remaining ½ cup Parmesan cheese. Spread about 1 cup of the sauce in an ungreased 3-quart shallow baking dish or 13 x 9 x 2-inch baking pan. Arrange cooked lasagna noodles on sauce in dish. Spread with one-third of the artichoke mixture and one-third of the remaining sauce. Sprinkle with ½ cup of the mozzarella mixture. Repeat layers twice.

6 Bake, uncovered, for 35 to 40 minutes or until edges are bubbly and top is lightly browned. Let stand for 15 minutes.

PER SERVING 350 CAL; 21 g FAT (10 g SAT); 64 mg CHOL; 470 mg SODIUM; 25 g CARB; 3 g FIBER; 16 g PRO

Cheese Fondue Casserole

Cheesy-rich casseroles are often the first creations to disappear from potluck tables. This little number—studded with chunks of nutty Swiss cheese—will ensure that you go home with a totally empty casserole dish.

MAKES 8 servings **PREP** 30 minutes
BAKE 35 minutes at 350°F

    Nonstick cooking spray
 3 cups dried elbow macaroni (12 ounces)
 3 cups shredded Swiss cheese* (12 ounces)
 2½ cups shredded Gruyère cheese* (10 ounces)
 5 tablespoons all-purpose flour
 3 cloves garlic, minced
 2 cups chicken broth
 ¾ cup dry white wine
    Salt
    Black pepper
 8 ounces Swiss cheese, cubed
 1¾ cups crushed saltine crackers (36)
 3 tablespoons butter, cut up

1 Preheat oven to 350°F. Coat a 3-quart casserole with cooking spray; set aside. Cook macaroni according to package directions; drain. Return macaroni to pan; set aside.

2 Meanwhile, in a large bowl combine shredded Swiss cheese, Gruyère cheese, flour, and garlic. Toss to combine. In a large saucepan heat broth and wine over medium heat just until bubbles form around edge of pan. Add cheese mixture, 1 cup at a time, whisking constantly after each addition until cheese is melted. (Mixture may not be completely smooth.) Do not boil. Remove from heat. Season to taste with pepper.

3 Pour cheese sauce over macaroni; stir gently to combine. Fold in cubed Swiss cheese. Spoon pasta mixture into prepared casserole. Sprinkle crushed crackers evenly over top; dot with butter.

4 Bake, uncovered, for 35 to 40 minutes or until bubbly and topping is golden.

*Note: For best results, shred the cheeses just before using. Purchased shredded cheese does not melt as well.

PER SERVING 568 CAL; 30 g FAT (18 g SAT); 93 mg CHOL; 603 mg SODIUM; 41 g CARB; 2 g FIBER; 30 g PRO

Italian Pinhead Torta

Inspired by her mother-in-law's rice torta, California cooking show host Laurie Figone transformed pinhead oats into the Italian-inspired top winner of Bob's Red Mill Steel Cut Oats Recipe Contest in Portland, Oregon—and joined Bob's Red Mill team on a journey to the Scottish Highlands to compete in the 19th Annual Golden Spurtle World Porridge Championship. The championship—honoring a 15th-century wooden stirring tool that resembles an ergonomically contoured dowel—drew contestants from around the world. In addition to the trip of a lifetime, Laurie won a $2,500 cash.

MAKES 12 servings **PREP** 25 minutes **STAND** 15 minutes **COOK** 15 minutes

1	ounce dried portobello mushrooms
1½	cups boiling water
1½	cups Bob's Red Mill Steel Cut Oats
6	tablespoons butter
1	cup diced onion (1 large)
1	cup coarsely shredded zucchini
½	cup diced dried tomatoes in olive oil, drained
6	eggs, room temperature
½	cup chopped fresh oregano
1	teaspoon garlic salt with parsley
1	cup shredded Parmesan cheese
	Freshly shredded Parmesan cheese

1 In a medium bowl combine dried mushrooms and boiling water; let stand for 10 minutes. Using a slotted spoon remove mushrooms, reserving liquid. Squeeze dry and chop the mushrooms; set aside. Stir the oats into the reserved mushroom liquid and let stand for 10 minutes.

2 In a large skillet heat 2 tablespoons of the butter over medium heat. Add onion; cook and stir until onions are translucent.

3 While onion is cooking, heat 2 tablespoons of the butter in a large saucepan over medium-high heat. Add soaked steel cut oats and stir constantly for 2 to 3 minutes or until liquid has evaporated; remove from heat. Add onion mixture, mushrooms, zucchini, and dried tomatoes; stir well.

4 In a large mixing bowl beat eggs; add oregano, garlic salt, and Parmesan cheese. Stir into oat mixture.

5 In the same large skillet heat remaining butter over medium-high heat. Pour in oat mixture and cover. Cook, covered, for 10 minutes or until cooked through. Remove lid and invert skillet onto a serving plate. Sprinkle with shredded Parmesan cheese.

PER SERVING 217 CAL; 12 g **FAT** (6 g **SAT**); 115 mg **CHOL**; 319 mg **SODIUM**; 19 g **CARB**; ; 3 g **FIBER**; 10 g **PRO**

Three-Cheese Beer Soup

Consider transferring this thick, rich soup to a warmed slow cooker before transporting to the potluck. Newer models even come with clever clasps that secure the lid tightly to the crock, making traveling with soup safe and secure.

MAKES 10 servings **START TO FINISH** 45 minutes

- 1½ **cups shredded sharp cheddar cheese (6 ounces)**
- 1¼ **cups shredded white cheddar cheese (5 ounces)**
- ¼ **cup butter**
- ½ **cup finely chopped onion (1 medium)**
- ½ **cup finely chopped carrot (1 medium)**
- ¼ **cup thinly sliced green onions (2)**
- 2 **cloves garlic, minced**
- ½ **cup all-purpose flour**
- ½ **teaspoon dry mustard**
- 5 **cups chicken broth**
- 1 **12-ounce bottle beer**
- 1 **cup whipping cream**
- 1½ **cups frozen diced hash brown potatoes**
- 1½ **cups small broccoli florets**
- 10 **slices bacon, crisp-cooked, drained, and chopped**
- ⅓ **cup grated Parmesan or Romano cheese**
- ½ **teaspoon bottled hot pepper sauce**
- ½ **teaspoon Worcestershire sauce**

1 Allow cheddar cheeses to stand at room temperature for 30 minutes. Meanwhile, in a 4-quart Dutch oven heat butter over medium heat until melted. Add ½ cup onion, carrot, green onions, and garlic. Cook for 8 to 10 minutes or until vegetables are tender, stirring occasionally.

2 Stir in flour and dry mustard (mixture will be thick). Gradually stir in broth. Cook and stir until bubbly. Add beer and whipping cream; stir in hash brown potatoes and broccoli. Bring to boiling; reduce heat. Simmer, uncovered, for 5 minutes, stirring occasionally.

3 Gradually add cheddar cheeses, stirring after each addition until cheeses are melted. Stir in bacon, Parmesan cheese, hot pepper sauce, and Worcestershire sauce.

PER SERVING 390 **CAL**; 29 g **FAT** (17 g **SAT**); 90 mg **CHOL**; 964 mg **SODIUM**; 16 g **CARB**; 1 g **FIBER**; 15 g **PRO**

Chicken and Sausage Gumbo

Roux—pronounced ROO—is a thickener used in authentic Cajun fare. You will know when the roux is ready—not only will it take on a dark reddish color, but it will smell sweet and nutty.

MAKES 10 servings **PREP** 45 minutes **COOK** 1 hour

- 1 **cup all-purpose flour**
- ⅔ **cup vegetable oil**
- 1 **cup sliced celery (2 stalks)**
- 1 **cup chopped green sweet pepper (1 large)**
- ½ **cup chopped onion (1 medium)**
- 2 **cloves garlic, minced**
- 8 **ounces cooked smoked sausage links, cut into 1-inch pieces**
- 8 **ounces cooked andouille sausage links, cut into ½-inch pieces**
- 2 **pounds meaty chicken pieces (breast halves, thighs, and drumsticks), skinned if desired**
- 5 **cups water**
- 1 **teaspoon salt**
- ¼ **to ½ teaspoon cayenne pepper**
- ¼ **teaspoon black pepper**
- 5 **cups hot cooked rice (optional)**

1 For roux, in a large heavy Dutch oven stir together flour and oil until smooth. Cook over medium-high heat for 5 minutes. Reduce heat to medium. Cook and stir for 10 to 15 minutes or until roux is reddish brown in color (the deeper the color, the richer and more flavorful the gumbo). Stir in celery, sweet pepper, onion, and garlic; cook for 5 minutes more, stirring occasionally. Add sausages; cook until sausages are lightly browned, stirring occasionally.

2 Add chicken, the water, salt, cayenne pepper, and black pepper. Bring to boiling; reduce heat. Simmer, covered, about 1 hour or until chicken is no longer pink (170°F for breasts; 180°F for thighs and drumsticks). Skim off fat.

3 Remove chicken from Dutch oven. When chicken is cool enough to handle, remove meat from bones; discard skin (if present) and bones. Coarsely chop chicken and return to gumbo. Cook for 2 to 3 minutes or until chicken is heated through. If desired, serve with rice.

PER SERVING 460 **CAL**; 34 g **FAT** (9 g **SAT**); 72 mg **CHOL**; 961 mg **SODIUM**; 12 g **CARB**; 1 g **FIBER**; 25 g **PRO**

CHICKEN AND SAUSAGE GUMBO

Five-Herb Roasted Carrots and Potatoes

New potatoes vary a great deal in weight and size. When selecting the spuds for this herb-enhanced roast, take care to choose same-size potatoes so they roast evenly.

MAKES 18 servings **PREP** 25 minutes **BAKE** 45 minutes at 400°F

6	pounds tiny new potatoes
6	medium carrots, cut into bite-size pieces
⅓	cup snipped fresh chives
2	butter or margarine, melted
⅓	cup olive oil
2	tablespoons snipped fresh oregano
2	tablespoons snipped fresh parsley
2	snipped fresh rosemary
8	cloves garlic, minced (optional)
1	tablespoon snipped fresh sage
1½	teaspoons salt
½	teaspoon freshly ground black pepper

1 Preheat oven to 400°F. Grease two shallow roasting pans. Cut unpeeled potatoes into quarters. Place in prepared pans. Add carrots.

2 In a small bowl combine chives, melted butter, oil, oregano, parsley, rosemary, garlic (if desired), sage, salt, and pepper. Drizzle over potato mixture; toss gently to coat. Cover pans with foil. Bake for 30 minutes. Stir potato mixture. Bake, uncovered, for 15 to 20 minutes more or until potatoes are tender.

PER SERVING 202 **CAL**; 9 g **FAT** (3 g **SAT**); 11 mg **CHOL**; 254 mg **SODIUM**; 28 g **CARB**; 3 g **FIBER**; 4 g **PRO**

Herbed Yukon Gold and Sweet Potato Gratin

Any medium-starch gold-flesh potatoes are ideal for this recipe. Yellow Finns are another excellent variety.

MAKES 8 servings **PREP** 25 minutes **BAKE** 1 hour 15 minutes at 350°F **STAND** 10 minutes

½   **cup chopped green onions (2)**
1   **tablespoon snipped fresh sage**
1   **tablespoon snipped fresh thyme**
3   **cloves garlic, minced**
1   **teaspoon salt**
½   **teaspoon black pepper**
1½ **pounds sweet potatoes, peeled and thinly sliced**
1½ **pounds Yukon gold potatoes, peeled and thinly sliced**
½   **cup finely shredded Gruyère cheese or Swiss cheese**
¼   **cup finely shredded Parmesan cheese**
½   **cup chicken broth**
½   **cup whipping cream**
     Fresh sage leaves (optional)

1 Preheat oven to 350°F. Grease a 13 x 9 x 2-inch baking dish; set aside. In a small bowl combine green onions, snipped sage, thyme, garlic, salt, and pepper; set aside.

2 Layer half of the sweet potatoes and half of the Yukon gold potatoes in the prepared baking dish, alternating rows if desired. Top with half of the herb mixture; sprinkle with half of the Gruyère cheese and half of the Parmesan cheese. Repeat layers. Pour broth and cream over layers in dish.

3 Cover with foil. Bake for 1 hour. Uncover and continue baking for 15 to 20 minutes or until potatoes are tender and top is lightly browned. Let stand for 10 to 15 minutes before serving. If desired, garnish with sage leaves.

PER SERVING 240 **CAL**; 9 g **FAT** (5 g **SAT**); 32 mg **CHOL**; 480 mg **SODIUM**; 34 g **CARB**; 5 g **FIBER**; 7 g **PRO**

Home-Style Green Bean Bake

This is it—the Thanksgiving classic. But it's far too tasty to be served only once a year.

MAKES 12 servings **PREP** 15 minutes **BAKE** 45 minutes at 350°F

- **2** **10.75-ounce cans condensed cream of mushroom soup or cream of celery soup**
- **1** **cup shredded cheddar cheese or American cheese**
- **2** **2-ounce jars sliced pimiento, drained (optional)**
- **6** **14.5-ounce cans French-cut green beans or cut green beans, drained, or 6 cups frozen French-cut green beans or cut green beans, thawed**
- **2** **8-ounce cans french-fried onions**

1 Preheat oven to 350°F. In a large bowl combine soup, cheese, and, if desired, pimiento. Stir in green beans. Transfer bean mixture to a 3-quart casserole.

2 Bake for 40 minutes. Remove from oven and stir; sprinkle with french-fried onions. Bake about 5 minutes more or until heated through.

PER SERVING 194 **CAL**; 12 g **FAT** (3 g **SAT**); 12 mg **CHOL**; 1,180 mg **SODIUM**; 16 g **CARB**; 2 g **FIBER**; 6 g **PRO**

Chile-Cheddar Casserole Bread

Homemade breads are a rarely found treasure at potluck events. But with this Tex-Mex-inspired recipe and only 20 minutes of hands-on time, you can be the one that delivers the bounty.

MAKES 8 to 12 servings **PREP** 20 minutes **RISE** 1 hour **BAKE** 45 minutes at 350°F **STAND** 10 minutes **COOL** 20 minutes

¼ **cup warm hot-style vegetable juice (105°F to 115°F)**

1 **package active dry yeast**

1 **cup sour cream**

¼ **cup finely chopped onion**

2 **eggs**

2 **tablespoons sugar**

1 **teaspoon salt**

½ **teaspoon ancho chile powder**

2½ **cups all-purpose flour**

1⅓ **cups finely shredded sharp cheddar cheese (about 5 ounces)**

1 **4-ounce can fire-roasted diced green chiles, undrained**

   Sliced green onion (optional)

1 In a large mixing bowl combine vegetable juice and yeast; let stand until mixture is foamy. Add sour cream, onion, eggs, sugar, salt, ancho chile powder, and 1 cup of the flour. Beat with an electric mixer on medium for 2 minutes. Using a wooden spoon, stir in the remaining 1½ cups flour, 1 cup of the cheese, and the green chiles until a soft, sticky dough forms.

2 Transfer dough to a greased 2-quart oval or rectangular baking dish. Cover; let rise in a warm place until double in size (1 to 1½ hours).

3 Preheat oven to 350°F. Bake for 40 minutes; remove from oven and sprinkle with remaining cheese. Return to oven; bake for 5 minutes more. Let dish stand on a wire rack for 10 minutes. Remove bread from dish. Let cool on wire rack for 20 minutes before serving. If desired, garnish with sliced green onion and additional chile powder.

PER SERVING 203 **CAL**; 8 g **FAT** (5 g **SAT**); 57 mg **CHOL**; 340 mg **SODIUM**; 24 g **CARB**; 1 g **FIBER**; 8 g **PRO**

Spicy Apricot and Sausage Braid

This spectacular-looking, scrumptious-tasting loaf is as perfect for an evening potluck as it is for a brunch or an after-church get-together.

MAKES 1 servings **PREP** 1 hour **RISE** 1 hour + 40 minutes **STAND** 10 minutes **BAKE** 20 minutes at 350°F

- **4 ounces andouille sausage, finely chopped**
- **½ cup finely chopped dried apricots**
- **½ to 1 teaspoon crushed red pepper**
- **½ cup snipped fresh cilantro**
- **2 tablespoons honey**
- **3 to 3½ cups all-purpose flour**
- **1 package active dry yeast**
- **1 teaspoon kosher salt**
- **⅔ cup warm water (105°F to 115°F)**
- **2 eggs, lightly beaten**
- **¼ cup olive oil**
- **1 egg, lightly beaten**
- **1 teaspoon water**

1 In a large nonstick skillet cook sausage over medium-high heat until it starts to brown. Stir in apricots and crushed red pepper. Cook and stir for 1 minute. Stir in cilantro and honey. Remove from heat; cool.

2 Meanwhile, in a large bowl combine 1 cup of the flour, the yeast, and salt. Add the ⅔ cup warm water, the 2 eggs, and the oil. Beat with an electric mixer on low to medium for 30 seconds, scraping sides of bowl constantly. Beat on high for 3 minutes. Stir in sausage mixture. Using a wooden spoon, stir in as much of the remaining flour as you can.

3 Turn dough out onto a lightly floured surface. Knead in enough of the remaining flour to make a soft dough that is smooth and elastic (3 to 5 minutes total). Shape dough into a ball. Place in a lightly greased bowl, turning once to grease surface. Cover; let rise in a warm place until double in size (about 1 hour).

4 Punch dough down. Turn dough out onto a lightly floured surface; divide dough into three portions. Cover; let rest for 10 minutes. Meanwhile, line a large baking sheet with parchment paper.

5 Gently roll each dough portion into a 16-inch-long rope. Place the ropes 1 inch apart on the prepared baking sheet; braid. Cover. Let rise in a warm place until nearly double in size (about 40 minutes).

6 Preheat oven to 350°F. In a small bowl combine the 1 egg and the 1 teaspoon water; brush over braid. Bake for 20 to 25 minutes or until loaf sounds hollow when lightly tapped. Cool on a wire rack.

PER SERVING 158 **CAL**; 5 g **FAT** (1 g **SAT**); 45 mg **CHOL**; 188 mg **SODIUM**; 23 g **CARB**; 1 g **FIBER**; 5 g **PRO**

Layered California-Style BLT Salad

Perfectly ripe avocados are essential to making this stunning layered salad a sure success. Try this trick when selecting avocados: Using your thumbnail, flick the brown spot on the avocado's stem end. If it won't budge, the avocado is not ready. If you can peel it up and see bright green beneath, it is just right. If there is no brown spot, it is too ripe.

MAKES 12 servings **PREP** 35 minutes **BAKE** 20 minutes at 300°F **CHILL** 8 hours

- 2 12-ounce packages applewood-smoked bacon
- 1 recipe Garlicky Focaccia Croutons
- 4 cups shredded romaine lettuce
- 4 cups baby spinach leaves
- 6 medium red and/or yellow heirloom tomatoes, cored, quartered, and sliced ½ inch thick (3 cups)
- 1 recipe Dilled Avocado Dressing

1 In a very large skillet cook bacon in batches over medium heat until crisp. Drain bacon on paper towels. When cool, coarsely crumble or chop bacon. Set aside.

2 In a 3- to 4-quart glass bowl layer half the Garlicky Focaccia Croutons, half the romaine, half the spinach, half the tomato slices, and half the bacon. Spread half the Dilled Avocado Dressing over the bacon, sealing dressing to the edge of the bowl. Repeat layering, ending with the dressing. Cover bowl tightly with plastic wrap. Chill for up to 8 hours.

Garlicky Focaccia Croutons: Preheat oven to 300°F. In a large bowl combine 3 cups of ½-inch cubes garlic focaccia and 2 tablespoons olive oil; toss to coat. Spread bread cubes evenly in a 15 x 10 x 1-inch baking pan. Bake about 20 minutes or until cubes are crisp, stirring once; cool. If desired, store croutons in an airtight container at room temperature for up to 3 days. Makes 2 cups.

Dilled Avocado Dressing: In a blender or food processor combine 1 ripe avocado, halved, seeded, peeled, and mashed (about 1 cup); ½ cup mayonnaise; ½ cup sour cream; 3 tablespoons freshly squeezed lemon juice; 3 tablespoons snipped fresh dill; ¼ cup milk; ½ teaspoon garlic salt; and ¼ teaspoon black pepper. Cover and blend until smooth. Makes 2 cups.

PER SERVING 465 **CAL**; 44 g **FAT** (12 g **SAT**); 47 mg **CHOL**; 614 mg **SODIUM**; 11 g **CARB**; 4 g **FIBER**; 9 g **PRO**

Mediterranean Wild Rice Salad

When making this hearty salad, read the wild rice package carefully. If it is labeled "cultivated" wild rice, follow the recipe's cooking time. If you have true wild rice, check the rice for tenderness after about 25 minutes of cooking time.

MAKES 12 servings **PREP** 30 minutes **COOK** 51 minutes **CHILL** 2 hours

- **3 cups reduced-sodium chicken broth**
- **1 cup uncooked wild rice, rinsed and drained**
- **1 recipe Moroccan Vinaigrette**
- **4 ounces thinly sliced pancetta, cut into thin strips**
- **1 15-ounce can garbanzo beans (chickpeas), rinsed and drained**
- **1 cup chopped orange sweet pepper (1 large)**
- **1 cup grape tomatoes, halved**
- **½ cup chopped red onion (1 medium)**
- **½ cup pimiento-stuffed green olives, halved**
- **½ cup golden raisins**
- **⅓ cup snipped fresh cilantro**
- **2 tablespoons capers, rinsed and drained**
- **½ cup pine nuts, toasted (see note, page 123)**
- **Fresh oregano sprigs (optional)**

1 In a large saucepan combine chicken broth and wild rice. Bring to boiling; reduce heat. Cover and simmer for 45 to 50 minutes or until just tender; drain if necessary. Transfer rice to a large bowl. Fluff rice with a fork and let cool about 10 minutes. Stir in Moroccan Vinaigrette while rice is still warm. Set aside.

2 Meanwhile, in a large skillet cook pancetta over medium heat about 6 minutes or until pancetta is crisp and browned, stirring frequently. Using a slotted spoon, transfer pancetta to paper towels to drain. When cool, transfer to a resealable plastic bag and chill.

3 Add garbanzo beans, pepper, tomatoes, onion, olives, raisins, cilantro, and capers to rice. Toss gently to combine. Cover and chill for 2 hours.

4 Just before serving, stir salad well. Add pancetta and pine nuts to salad; toss gently to combine. If desired, garnish with oregano sprigs.

Moroccan Vinaigrette: In a screw-top jar combine ½ cup red wine vinegar, 3 tablespoons minced shallot, 2 tablespoons snipped fresh Italian parsley, 2 tablespoons olive oil, 1 tablespoon lemon juice, 1 clove minced garlic, ½ teaspoon paprika, ¼ teaspoon cayenne pepper, and ¼ teaspoon ground cumin. Cover and shake well.

PER SERVING 229 **CAL**; 11 g **FAT** (2 g **SAT**); 7 mg **CHOL**; 552 mg **SODIUM**; 27 g **CARB**; 4 g **FIBER**; 7 g **PRO**

Creamy Hot Chicken Salad

This American classic—an often-shared recipe in the '60s—is as wonderful now as it was then. Be extra thrifty by saving the potato chip crumbs from the bottoms of bags in a tightly sealed container in your freeze. Before you know it, you'll have enough to top this creamy concoction.

MAKES 12 servings **PREP** 25 minutes **BAKE** 25 minutes at 400°F

¾ **cup coarsely crushed potato chips**

½ **cup chopped pecans**

6 **cups chopped cooked chicken**

2 **cups shredded cheddar cheese (8 ounces)**

2 **cups chopped celery (4 stalks)**

1 **cup chopped red and/or yellow sweet pepper (1 large)**

¼ **cup sliced green onions (1)**

1 **10.75-ounce can condensed cream of chicken soup**

1 **cup mayonnaise**

1 **8-ounce carton sour cream**

1 **teaspoon dried thyme or basil, crushed**

¼ **teaspoon black pepper**

Coarsely crushed potato chips (optional)

1 **recipe Caramelized Red Onion (optional)**

1 Preheat oven to 400°F. In a small bowl combine potato chips and pecans. Set aside.

2 In a large bowl stir together the chicken, cheese, celery, sweet pepper, and green onions. In a medium bowl stir together the soup, mayonnaise, sour cream, thyme, and black pepper. Fold soup mixture into chicken mixture. Transfer to a 3-quart rectangular baking dish. Sprinkle evenly with potato chip mixture.

3 Bake, uncovered, for 25 to 30 minutes or until heated through and bubbly. If desired, top with additional crushed potato chips and Caramelized Red Onions.

PER SERVING 478 **CAL**; 37 g **FAT** (12 g **SAT**); 100 mg **CHOL**; 554 mg **SODIUM**; 8 g **CARB**; 1 g **FIBER**; 27 g **PRO**

Caramelized Red Onion: Cut 1 small red onion into thin wedges. In a small saucepan cook onion, covered, in 1 tablespoon hot butter over low heat about 15 minutes or until tender and golden, stirring occasionally.

CHAPTER 8
handheld favorites

Delicious takes on sandwiches, wraps, pizza, and pocket pies.

SAUCY MEATBALL SANDWICHES

Jambalaya Pizza

Instead of the typical yeast bread crust, this clever concoction uses a spicy mixture of rice, egg, and pepper Jack cheese as its foundation. Although any smoked sausage will work, see if you can find smoky, garlicky Andouille sausage to play up the recipe's Cajun roots.

MAKES 6 to 8 servings **PREP** 30 minutes
BAKE 30 minutes at 450°F/425°

3	cups cooked long grain rice, cooled
2	eggs, lightly beaten
1	cup finely shredded pepper Jack cheese
¼	cup chopped celery
¼	cup chopped green sweet pepper
¼	cup chopped onion
1	tablespoon butter
1	clove garlic, minced
½	cup thinly sliced smoked cooked sausage
½	cup diced cooked ham
½	cup coarsely chopped cooked shrimp
1	16-ounce jar chunky salsa, drained (1⅓ cups)
¾	cup shredded mozzarella cheese (3 ounces)

1 Preheat oven to 450°F. In large bowl combine rice, eggs, and pepper Jack cheese. Lightly coat a 12-inch pizza pan with nonstick cooking spray. Spread rice mixture evenly in pan. Bake for 20 minutes. Remove from oven; reduce oven temperature to 425°F.

2 For topping, in a large skillet cook celery, green pepper, and onion in hot butter over medium heat for 8 to 10 minutes or until tender, stirring occasionally. Stir in garlic, sausage, ham, and shrimp. Cook until heated through.

3 Spread drained salsa over rice crust, leaving a ½-inch border. Spread vegetable-meat mixture over salsa. Sprinkle with mozzarella cheese. Bake for 10 to 15 minutes or until heated through and cheese is melted. Cut into pieces to serve.

PER SERVING 364 **CAL**; 18 g **FAT** (10 g **SAT**); 145 mg **CHOL**; 1,004 mg **SODIUM**; 29 g **CARB**; 2 g **FIBER**; 19 g **PRO**

Greek-Style Pizza

If you've ever driven by an Indian grocery store and wondered what's inside, use naan—a classic Indian flatbread—as an excuse to stop in. You'll not only find naan but a wealth of other fascinating ingredients, including commonly used spices, at a fraction of the cost of their supermarket counterparts.

MAKES 4 servings **START TO FINISH** 25 minutes

2	cups packaged refrigerated diced potatoes with onion
1	tablespoon olive oil
4	naan flatbreads or pita rounds
	Olive oil
4	ounces crumbled feta cheese with garlic and herb
2	cups packaged fresh spinach
12	ounces thinly sliced deli lower-sodium roast beef
	Sliced baby sweet peppers (optional)
	Crushed red pepper (optional)

1 In a large skillet cook potatoes in the 1 tablespoon oil over medium heat for 5 minutes or until tender; set aside.

2 Meanwhile, heat broiler. Place flatbreads on an extra-large baking sheet; lightly brush bread tops with oil. Top with half of the cheese. Broil 3 to 4 inches from the heat for 2 to 3 minutes or until cheese begins to melt. Top barely melted cheese with spinach, roast beef, potatoes, and remaining cheese.

3 Broil for 3 to 5 minutes more or until heated through. Drizzle with additional olive oil, then, if desired, top with pepper slices and crushed red pepper.

PER SERVING 555 **CAL**; 24 g **FAT** (11 g **SAT**); 96 mg **CHOL**; 1,243 mg **SODIUM**; 57 g **CARB**; 1 g **FIBER**; 30 g **PRO**

GREEK-STYLE PIZZA

Chorizo-Pepper Hand Pies

If you're unable to find queso fresco—a fresh, milky, and mild Mexican-style cheese—crumbled feta or dabs of ricotta cheese will do the trick.

PREP 45 minutes   **COOK** 17 minutes   **BAKE** 12 minutes at 400°F

1	**tablespoon extra virgin olive oil**
¼	**cup finely chopped red onion**
2	**cloves garlic, minced**
½	**of a yellow sweet pepper, seeded and finely chopped**
5	**ounces uncooked chorizo sausage**
½	**cup chopped tomato, fresh or canned**
1	**teaspoon dried oregano, crushed**
½	**teaspoon ground cumin**
4	**ounces grated queso fresco (¾ cup)**
1	**17.3-ounce package frozen puff pastry sheets (2 sheets), thawed**
1	**egg yolk, lightly beaten**
1	**tablespoon milk**
1	**recipe Sweet Pepper Topping (optional)**
	Taco sauce or salsa (optional)

1 For filling, heat the oil in a large skillet over medium heat. Add onion, garlic, and sweet pepper and cook 7 minutes, stirring occasionally until tender. Add chorizo, stirring occasionally, and breaking up sausage until sausage is no longer pink, 5 minutes. Drain fat. Return to heat and add tomato, oregano, and cumin to filling. Simmer, uncovered, 5 to 8 minutes or until filling is almost dry. Season with salt and black pepper. Let cool. Add queso fresco and stir to combine.

2 Preheat oven to 400°F. On a floured surface with a floured rolling pin roll puff pastry to ⅛-inch thickness. With a 3½-inch round cookie cutter, cut 24 circles. Place 1 tablespoon filling in center of each circle. Combine beaten egg yolk with milk. Brush edges of half the circle with egg wash. Fold over circle to enclose filling; pinch edges together to seal. Brush tops with egg wash. Place on an ungreased baking sheet; bake 12 minutes or until golden brown.

3 Serve warm topped with Sweet Pepper Topper and taco sauce for dipping if desired.

PER SERVING 164 **CAL**; 11 g **FAT** (3 g **SAT**); 16 mg **CHOL**; 234 mg **SODIUM**; 12 g **CARB**; 1 g **FIBER**; 4 g **PRO**

Sweet Pepper Topping: In small bowl combine 1 cup chopped yellow and/or orange sweet pepper, ⅓ cup chopped pitted ripe olives, and ¼ cup chopped fresh parsley.

Barbecue Pasties

Pasties—handheld cabbage and potato pies once prepared by Cornish wives for their miner husbands—take on the sweet and spicy flavors of the American South. To save time, you can use a container of refrigerated preshredded beef or pork.

MAKES 12 servings **PREP** 40 minutes **BAKE** 20 minutes at 375°F

- **1** recipe Pastry for Double-Crust Pie*
- **¾** cup chopped green sweet pepper (1 medium)
- **½** cup chopped sweet onion (1 small)
- **1** tablespoon vegetable oil
- **1½** cups shredded cooked pork, beef, chicken, or turkey
- **½** cup bottled barbecue sauce
- **1** cup shredded sharp cheddar cheese or Monterey Jack cheese with jalapeño peppers (4 ounces)
  Milk
  Warmed barbecue sauce and/or sweet-hot mustard

1 Preheat oven to 375°F. Prepare Pastry for Double-Crust Pie. Divide dough into two portions. On a lightly floured surface use your hands to slightly flatten one pastry portion. Roll pastry from center to edges into a circle 13½ to 14 inches in diameter. Cut five 5-inch circles. Reroll scraps to cut a sixth circle. Repeat with remaining dough half for a total of twelve 5-inch circles.

2 For filling, in a medium skillet cook sweet pepper and onion in hot oil over medium heat about 4 minutes or until vegetables are tender. Stir in pork and the ½ cup barbecue sauce.

3 Spoon about 2 tablespoons of the meat mixture onto half of each pastry circle. Top with a rounded tablespoon shredded cheese. Lightly moisten edge of pastry with milk. Fold pastry over filling. Seal edges by crimping with a fork. Cut slits in pastry to allow steam to escape. Brush pasties with a little additional milk. Place on an extra-large ungreased baking sheet (or on 2 medium baking sheets).

4 Bake for 20 to 25 minutes or until golden brown. Cool slightly on wire racks. Serve warm with additional barbecue sauce and/or sweet-hot mustard for dipping.

Pastry for Double-Crust Pie: In a large bowl stir together 2½ cups all-purpose flour and 1 teaspoon salt. Using a pastry blender, cut in ½ cup shortening and ¼ cup cut-up butter until pieces are pea size. Sprinkle 1 tablespoon ice water over part of the flour mixture; toss gently with a fork. Push moistened dough to side of bowl. Repeat with additional ice water, 1 tablespoon at a time (½ to ⅔ cup

total), until all the flour mixture is moistened. Gather pastry into a ball and gently knead until it holds together.

*Note: To save time, use one 15-ounce package rolled refrigerated unbaked piecrust (2) instead of the homemade pastry. Let stand according to package directions. Roll and cut as directed.

PER SERVING 348 **CAL**; 20 g **FAT** (8 g **SAT**); 38 mg **CHOL**; 586 mg **SODIUM**; 31 g **CARB**; 1 g **FIBER**; 11 g **PRO**

The Dreamiest Sandwich

Longtime Scio, Oregon, grandmother Frances Benthin has been fond of grilled cheese sandwiches for decades. Some of her best memories date back to World War II, when her girlfriends and servicemen dates would close down the dance hall, then gather at her house to feast on grilled cheese sandwiches—called Dream Sandwiches at the time. Her recipe contest successes are many, including winning a Harley-Davidson motorcycle and a trip to the Super Bowl. Her lengthy experience and an ingenious recipe captured the judges' taste buds at the 2nd Annual Tillamook Cheese Factory Grilled Cheese Contest, where she took First Place honors, won $500, a huge basket of cheese, and bragging rights.

MAKES 2 servings **PREP** 15 minutes **COOK** 3 minutes

- ½   **chopped roasted red sweet pepper**
- ¼   **cup diced prosciutto**
- ¼   **cup Tillamook pepper Jack cheese, diced (2 ounces)**
- 2   **tablespoons Tillamook premium sour cream**
- 1   **tablespoon dill pickle relish**
- 2   **teaspoons Dijon mustard**
- 4   **ounces thinly sliced Tillamook vintage white extra-sharp cheddar cheese**
- 4   **thick slices hazelnut bread, walnut bread, or whole wheat bread**
- 4   **teaspoons Tillamook unsalted butter, room temperature**

1 In a small bowl combine the sweet pepper, prosciutto, pepper Jack cheese, sour cream, pickle relish, and mustard; mix well. Spread filling onto 2 bread slices; top with cheddar cheese. Top with the remaining bread slices. Butter the top of the bread with 2 teaspoons of the butter.

2 Heat a large skillet over medium-high heat and melt the remaining butter until hot but not smoking. Place sandwiches, butter sides up, in the skillet and grill for 2 to 3 minutes or until browned. Carefully turn sandwich and grill on the opposite side for 1 to 2 minutes more or until cheese is beginning to melt.

3 To serve, slice sandwiches diagonally in half.

PER SERVING 657 **CAL**; 41 g **FAT** (22 g **SAT**); 118 mg **CHOL**; 1,251 mg **SODIUM**; 42 g **CARB**; 3 g **FIBER**; 28 g **PRO**

The Strawberry Hunger Abater

Jennifer Zuk—of Burnaby, British Columbia—became $25,000 richer when her Strawberry Hunger Abater Sandwich won Grand Prize in the 2012 Mezzetta Make That Sandwich! Contest. Jennifer intended to enter the contest but did not come up with her winning idea until she was so hungry while driving home from doing errands that she had to dig into the strawberries in her grocery bag. Her quick and easy recipe, which takes only 15 minutes to prepare, also earned her a trip for two to Napa Valley, California.

MAKES 2 servings **START TO FINISH** 15 minutes

2   **croissants**

¼   **cup mayonnaise**

1   **Mezzetta roasted red sweet pepper, drained**

2   **teaspoons Kona Coast Hawaiian honey mustard**

1½   **teaspoons soft goat cheese**

5   **to 6 large strawberries, sliced**

14   **Mezzetta pitted kalamata olives, halved**

¼   **cup thinly sliced almonds**

¼   **cup Mezzetta golden Greek pepperoncini, sliced**

14   **Mezzetta deli-sliced roasted sweet bell pepper strips, drained**

4   **to 8 large spinach leaves**

1 Slice the croissants horizontally. Set aside.

2 Puree the mayonnaise and roasted red pepper in a food processor. Spread croissants bottoms with honey mustard, then goat cheese. Top with sliced strawberries, then olives, almonds, pepperoncini, pepper strips, and spinach leaves.

3 Spread 2 tablespoons of the mayonnaise mixture on each top half of the croissants. Place on sandwiches.

PER SERVING 502 **CAL**; 35 g **FAT** (9 g **SAT**);46 mg **CHOL**; 861 mg **SODIUM**; 39 g **CARB**; 6 g **FIBER**; 9 g **PRO**

Antipasto Italian Panini

Grilled sandwiches are a great idea for sultry summer nights. Not only are they quick and easy to prepare, but grilling imbues them with a smoky, rich crispness enticing to weather-weary appetites.

MAKES 4 servings   **PREP** 20 minutes   **GRILL** 12 minutes

1	9- to 10-inch focaccia (about 1 pound)
2	tablespoons butter, softened
¼	cup olive tapenade and/or pesto
4	ounces sliced provolone cheese
3	ounces sliced salami
3	ounces sliced coppocola
4	pepperoncini
6	to 12 fresh basil leaves

1 Cut focaccia in half horizontally. If necessary, trim off the top and bottom of the focaccia halves to make each half about ¾ inch thick. Butter the outsides of the focaccia halves. Spread insides of focaccia halves with tapenade. Place half of the provolone on one of the focaccia halves. Top with salami, coppocola, pepperoncini, and basil leaves. Top with remaining provolone and remaining focaccia half.

2 Arrange medium-hot coals around the outer edge of a charcoal grill. Test for medium heat in the center of the grill. Place panino on a grill rack in the center of the grill. Place a baking sheet on top of the sandwich and weight it with two bricks. Cover and grill 12 to 16 minutes, turning once, or until bread is golden brown and cheese is melted. (For a gas grill, preheat grill. Reduce heat to medium. Adjust for indirect grilling. Place panino on a grill rack away from heat. Grill as above.) To serve, cut into wedges.

PER SERVING 604 **CAL**; 35 g **FAT** (13 g **SAT**); 78 mg **CHOL**; 1,912 mg **SODIUM**; 51 g **CARB**; 3 g **FIBER**; 25 g **PRO**

Pork Tenderloin Sandwiches

Making the homemade version of this fast food favorite takes—start to finish—only 25 minutes! Serve it with oven-fried sweet potatoes for a meal far more delicious than one you'll find at a drive-through.

MAKES 4 servings **START TO FINISH** 25 minutes

1 **pound pork tenderloin**
¼ **cup all-purpose flour**
¼ **teaspoon garlic salt**
¼ **teaspoon black pepper**
1 **egg**
1 **tablespoon milk**
½ **cup seasoned fine dry bread crumbs**
2 **tablespoons vegetable oil**
4 **large hamburger buns or kaiser rolls, split and toasted**
   Ketchup, mustard, onion slices, and/or dill pickle slices

1 Trim fat from meat. Cut meat crosswise into four pieces. Place each piece between two pieces of plastic wrap. Using the flat side of a meat mallet, pound meat lightly to about ¼-inch thickness. Remove plastic wrap.

2 In a shallow bowl combine flour, garlic salt, and pepper. In another shallow bowl whisk together egg and milk. Place bread crumbs in a third shallow bowl. Dip meat into flour mixture, turning to coat. Dip into egg mixture, then coat with bread crumbs.

3 In a large heavy skillet cook meat, half at a time if necessary, in hot oil over medium heat for 6 to 8 minutes or until meat is slightly pink in center and coating is brown, turning once.

4 Serve meat in buns with ketchup, mustard, onion, and/or dill pickles.

PER SERVING 424 **CAL**; 13 g **FAT** (3 g **SAT**); 127 mg **CHOL**; 776 mg **SODIUM**; 42 g **CARB**; 2 g **FIBER**; 33 g **PRO**

Tote-and-Slice Loaf Sandwich

Perfect picnic fare, this slice-and-eat, Italian-inspired sandwich is a summertime staple that will serve you well.

MAKES 6 servings **START TO FINISH** 25 minutes

- ¾ **cup dried tomatoes (not oil-packed)**
- 1 **pound Italian or French bread**
- ½ **of an 8-ounce package cream cheese, softened**
- ⅓ **cup basil pesto**
- 4 **ounces thinly sliced provolone cheese**
- 8 **ounces thinly sliced peppered or regular salami**
- 1 **fresh banana pepper or 8 bottled banana peppers, stemmed, seeded, and sliced**
- ½ **red onion, thinly sliced**
  Small salad peppers and/or pimiento-stuffed green olives (optional)

1 Place tomatoes in a small bowl. Add enough boiling water to cover and let stand for 10 minutes. Drain tomatoes and place in a food processor; cover and process until finely chopped. Or finely chop tomatoes by hand.

2 Split loaf in half horizontally. Remove some soft bread from the bottom half of the loaf, leaving a ½-inch shell.

3 Spread cream cheese evenly on cut sides of both bread halves. Spread the top half with dried tomatoes and the bottom half with pesto. On the bottom half layer provolone cheese, salami, banana peppers, and onion. Top with the loaf top, spread side down.

4 Tightly wrap loaf with plastic wrap. To serve, slice loaf crosswise into six sandwiches. If desired, spear salad peppers and/or olives with long toothpicks; insert a toothpick through each sandwich.

PER SERVING 588 **CAL**; 34 g **FAT** (14 g **SAT**); 69 mg **CHOL**; 1,645 mg **SODIUM**; 46 g **CARB**; 4 g **FIBER**; 24 g **PRO**

Beef and Red Onion Sandwiches

Add nothing more than some carrot sticks and a perfect piece of fruit to accompany this quick and easy sandwich—and a healthful, hearty dinner will be on the table in 20 minutes.

MAKES 4 servings **START TO FINISH** 20 minutes

- 8 **dried tomato strips or halves (not oil-packed)**
- 12 **ounces boneless beef sirloin steak, cut ¾ inch thick**
- 1 **small red onion, thinly sliced**
- 2 **tablespoons olive oil**
  Salt
  Black pepper
- 4 **square bagels or ciabatta rolls, split**
- ¼ **cup mayonnaise**
- 1 **cup mixed salad greens**

1 Preheat broiler. Place dried tomatoes in a small microwave-safe bowl; cover with water. Heat on high for 1 minute; drain.

2 Meanwhile, trim fat from meat. Brush meat and onion with oil. Place on the unheated rack of a broiler pan; sprinkle with salt and pepper. Broil 3 to 4 inches from the heat for 12 to 16 minutes or until desired doneness, turning once halfway through broiling. Thinly slice meat across the grain into bite-size strips.

3 Lightly spread split sides of bagels with mayonnaise. Layer bottoms of bagels with meat, onion, drained tomatoes, and salad greens. Replace bagel tops.

PER SERVING 451 **CAL**; 22 g **FAT** (4 g **SAT**); 51 mg **CHOL**; 681 mg **SODIUM**; 40 g **CARB**; 3 g **FIBER**; 26 g **PRO**

Saucy Meatball Sandwiches

Oven-roasting meatballs—rather than sauteing them in a skillet—saves time. Place meatballs on an oven-safe cooling rack placed over a baking sheet—the fat will fall onto the baking sheet, providing you with leaner meatballs.

MAKES 12 servings   **PREP** 5 minutes   **BAKE** 15 minutes at 350°F   **STAND** 1 minute

- **2**   **eggs, lightly beaten**
- **1½ cups soft whole wheat bread crumbs**
- **½   cup finely chopped onion (1 medium)**
- **½   teaspoon salt**
- **½   teaspoon dried Italian seasoning, crushed**
- **2   pounds lean ground beef**
- **2   26- to 28-ounce jars red pasta sauce**
- **12 hoagie buns or bratwurst buns**
- **½   cup grated Parmesan cheese**

1 Preheat oven to 350°F. In a large bowl combine eggs, bread crumbs, onion, salt, and Italian seasoning. Add ground beef; mix well. Shape into 48 meatballs. Arrange meatballs in a large roasting pan or 15 x 10 x 1-inch baking pan. Bake for 15 to 20 minutes or until done (160°F when tested with an instant-read thermometer). Drain well.

2 In a 4-quart Dutch oven combine the pasta sauce and meatballs. Heat through. Split buns or hollow out tops of unsplit buns. Spoon hot meatballs and sauce into buns. Spoon any remaining sauce over the meatballs. Sprinkle cheese over meatballs. If buns are split, top with bun halves. Let stand for 1 to 2 minutes before serving.

PER SERVING 599 **CAL**; 18 g **FAT** (6 g **SAT**); 86 mg **CHOL**; 1,351 mg **SODIUM**; 83 g **CARB**; 6 g **FIBER**; 29 g **PRO**

Chili Burgers

These bodacious, open-face burgers, dripping with spicy chili and melted cheddar, make a hot and hearty supper for a cold winter night.

MAKES 4 servings **START TO FINISH** 30 minutes

4	4-ounce ready-to-cook ground beef or turkey patties
½	teaspoon salt
	Dash black pepper
1	tablespoon vegetable oil
¼	cup chopped onion
1	clove garlic, minced
1	15-ounce can chili with beans
1	14.5-ounce can diced tomatoes, undrained
4	slices Texas toast, toasted
½	cup shredded cheddar cheese (2 ounces)

1 Sprinkle patties with salt and pepper. Heat a very large skillet over medium-high heat. Add patties; reduce heat to medium. Cook, uncovered, for 6 to 8 minutes or until juices run clear (160°F), turning once. Remove patties from skillet and keep warm. Drain fat from skillet; discard. Carefully wipe out skillet.

2 Add oil to skillet. Return skillet to heat. Add onion and garlic; cook over medium heat until tender. Stir in chili and undrained tomatoes. Bring to boiling; reduce heat. Simmer, uncovered, for 5 to 10 minutes or until desired consistency, stirring occasionally.

3 To serve, place patties on toast. Spoon chili over tops. Sprinkle with cheese.

PER SERVING 676 **CAL**; 43 g **FAT** (16 g **SAT**); 172 mg **CHOL**; 1,419 mg **SODIUM**; 39 g **CARB**; 5 g **FIBER**; 36 g **PRO**

CHAPTER 9
sweet
endings

Save room for dessert! These pages are packed with sweet indulgences.

SHORTBREAD BROWNIES

Sweet Potato Spice Flan Cake

Beginning with a master cake recipe previously adapted to feature four or five different flavors, Pat Harmon's inventive addition of sweet potatoes brought her Grand Prize honors—and a $1,000 prize—in the 7th Annual Sweet Rewards Recipe Contest, sponsored by the Louisiana Sweet Potato Commission and Louisiana Cookin' magazine. Winning recipe contests is nothing new to this talented cook and baker, who has also been a finalist in the National Beef Cook-Off three times.

MAKES 16 servings **PREP** 35 minutes **BAKE** 2 hours at 350°F **COOL** 15 minutes **CHILL** 6 hours

Nonstick cooking spray for baking
- ¾ **cup purchased caramel topping**
- ½ **teaspoon rum or brandy extract (optional)**
- 1 **15-ounce can Louisiana Cut sweet potatoes in light syrup, drained, reserving ½ cup syrup**
- 1 **2-layer-size spice cake mix**
- 1⅓ **cups water**
- 2 **tablespoons canola oil**
- 7 **eggs**
- 1 **8-ounce package cream cheese, softened and cubed**
- 1 **teaspoon pumpkin pie spice**
- ⅔ **cup sweetened condensed milk**
- ⅔ **cup evaporated milk**
- ¼ **cup chopped pecans, toasted (see tip, page 9)**

1 Preheat oven to 350°F. Coat a 15-cup fluted tube pan with nonstick cooking spray for baking. Place caramel topping in a small bowl; stir in rum extract, if using, and pour into the prepared pan. Place sweet potatoes and ½ cup reserved syrup in a food processor. Cover and process until smooth.

2 In a large mixing bowl combine cake mix, ½ cup of the sweet potato puree, water, oil, and 3 of the eggs. Beat with an electric mixer on medium for 2 minutes. Pour cake batter into pan over caramel topping. Set aside.

3 Place softened cream cheese cubes in a food processor. Cover and process until smooth. Add remaining sweet potato puree and pumpkin pie spice. Cover and process 15 to 20 seconds or until combined. Add condensed milk and evaporated milk to processor and process until smooth. Add remaining eggs, one at a time, processing just until combined and smooth. Carefully pour on batter in cake pan.

4 Coat a sheet of aluminum foil with the cooking spray and tightly cover the cake pan. Place the covered cake pan into a 13 x 9 x 2-inch baking pan. Pour very hot water into the baking pan until water reaches ½ inch up the sides of the cake pan. Bake for 2 hours.

5 Remove cake pan from water; let cool 15 minutes. Remove foil and invert cake onto a large cake platter. Cool completely at room temperature. Sprinkle pecans over top of cake. Cover and refrigerate 6 to 24 hours or until thoroughly chilled.

*Note: This cake requires a 15-cup fluted tube pan. A standard-size 12-cup fluted tube pan is too small. Look for this pan at specialty bake shops or online.

PER SERVING 353 **CAL**; 14 g **FAT** (6 g **SAT**); 105 mg **CHOL**; 380 mg **SODIUM**; 50 g **CARB**; 1 g **FIBER**; 7 g **PRO**

Triple-Citrus Pound Cake

A medley of three citrus fruits turns this cake into a sunny celebration. When removing the peel from grapefruit, limes, and oranges, be sure to remove just the very outer, colored layer—the pithy white flesh beneath it is bitter.

MAKES 16 servings **PREP** 20 minutes **BAKE** 40 minutes at 350°F **COOL** 10 minutes

½	**cup milk**
2	**teaspoons finely shredded grapefruit peel**
2	**teaspoons finely shredded lime peel**
2	**teaspoons finely shredded orange peel**
1	**tablespoon grapefruit juice**
1½	**cups sugar**
1¼	**cups butter, softened**
3	**eggs**
1	**teaspoon vanilla**
2¼	**cups all-purpose flour**
¾	**teaspoon baking powder**
½	**teaspoon baking soda**
¼	**teaspoon salt**
2	**tablespoons butter, melted**
1	**to 2 tablespoons orange juice**
¾	**cup powdered sugar**
	Finely shredded grapefruit peel, lime peel, and/or orange peel (optional)

1 Preheat oven to 350°F. Grease and flour a 10-inch fluted tube pan; set aside.

2 In a small bowl combine milk, the 2 teaspoons grapefruit peel, the 2 teaspoons lime peel, the 2 teaspoons orange peel, and the grapefruit juice. Mix well.

3 In a large bowl combine sugar and the 1¼ cups butter. Beat with an electric mixer on medium until light and fluffy. Add eggs, one at a time, beating well after each addition. Stir in vanilla.

4 In a medium mixing bowl combine flour, baking powder, baking soda, and salt. Alternately add flour mixture and milk mixture to butter mixture, beating just until moistened after each addition.

5 Spread batter into prepared pan. Bake for 40 to 45 minutes or until a toothpick inserted near the center of the cake comes out clean. Cool in pan on a wire rack for 10 minutes. Remove cake from pan; cool completely on wire rack.

6 To serve, in a small mixing bowl combine the 2 tablespoons melted butter and 1 tablespoon of the orange juice. Add powdered sugar; beat until smooth. If necessary, add enough of the remaining 1 tablespoon orange juice to make mixture drizzling consistency. Drizzle over cake. If desired, sprinkle with additional grated peel.

PER SERVING 319 **CAL**; 17 g **FAT** (10 g **SAT**); 82 mg **CHOL**; 228 mg **SODIUM**; 39 g **CARB**; 1 g **FIBER**; 3 g **PRO**

Stout Gingerbread with Lemony Hard Sauce

Mark this recipe for St. Patrick's Day, when Irish beers line the shelves. Stout beer gives this gingerbread an unusual deep flavor, and the dessert makes a wonderful end to a traditional corned beef dinner.

MAKES 12 servings **PREP** 25 minutes **STAND** 15 minutes **BAKE** 40 minutes at 350°F **COOL** 10 minutes

Nonstick spray for baking
¾ cup stout beer (such as Guinness)
2½ cups all-purpose flour
1 tablespoon ground ginger
2 teaspoons ground cinnamon
1½ teaspoons baking powder
½ teaspoon baking soda
½ teaspoon salt
¼ teaspoon freshly grated nutmeg or ⅛ teaspoon ground nutmeg
¼ teaspoon ground cardamom
1 cup butter, softened
1¼ cups packed brown sugar
3 eggs
1 cup mild-flavor molasses
1 tablespoon grated fresh ginger
1 tablespoon powdered sugar
1 recipe Lemony Hard Sauce

1 Preheat oven to 350°F. Generously coat a 10-inch fluted tube pan with spray for baking. Pour beer into a measuring cup and let stand at room temperature for 15 minutes. In a medium bowl stir together flour, ground ginger, cinnamon, baking powder, baking soda, salt, nutmeg, and cardamom; set aside.

2 In a large mixing bowl beat butter with an electric mixer on medium to high for 30 seconds. Add brown sugar. Beat until light and fluffy, scraping sides of bowl occasionally. Add eggs, one at a time, beating well after each addition. Stir in molasses and grated ginger. Alternately add flour mixture and beer in three additions, beating on medium just until combined after each addition. Pour batter into the prepared pan.

3 Bake for 40 to 50 minutes or until a wooden toothpick inserted near the center comes out clean. Cool in pan on a wire rack for 10 minutes. Remove cake from pan. Sprinkle with powdered sugar. Serve warm with Lemony Hard Sauce.

Lemony Hard Sauce: In a medium mixing bowl beat ¼ cup butter, softened, with an electric mixer on medium to high until light and fluffy. Beat in ¾ cup powdered sugar, 2 tablespoons lemon or orange liqueur, 2 teaspoons finely shredded lemon or orange peel, and 1 teaspoon vanilla until smooth.

PER SERVING 496 **CAL**; 21 g **FAT** (13 g **SAT**); 104 mg **CHOL**; 366 mg **SODIUM**; 73 g **CARB**; 1 g **FIBER**; 5 g **PRO**

Dutch Apple Cake with Caramel Glaze

This chunky apple cake will be just as marvelous when made with sweet apples as it is when prepared with tart baking apples, so the choice is yours.

MAKES 16 servings **PREP** 40 minutes **BAKE** 1 hour at 325°F

7	apples
3	cups unbleached all-purpose flour
1	teaspoon baking soda
1½	teaspoons ground cinnamon
1	teaspoon salt
½	teaspoon freshly grated nutmeg
3	eggs
1½	cups vegetable oil
1	cup packed brown sugar
1	cup granulated sugar
2½	teaspoons vanilla
1¼	cups chopped pecans
1	recipe Caramel Glaze

1 Preheat oven to 325°F. Butter and flour a 13 x 9 x 2-inch baking pan; set aside. Peel apples, quarter, core, and cut each quarter in half lengthwise, then crosswise (16 pieces from each apple).

2 In a medium bowl whisk together the flour, baking soda, cinnamon, salt, and nutmeg; set aside.

3 In a very large mixing bowl whisk eggs to combine. Whisk in oil, sugars, and vanilla until well blended. Gradually whisk in the flour mixture just until well blended. Fold apples and pecans into batter (batter will be thick and barely coat apples). Turn into prepared pan, spreading to edges of pan.

4 Bake about 1 hour or until a toothpick inserted in the center of the cake comes out clean. Remove from oven and cool on a wire rack while preparing glaze. Spoon Caramel Glaze over warm cake.

Caramel Glaze: In a medium skillet melt 6 tablespoons unsalted butter. Add ⅓ cup packed dark brown sugar, ⅓ cup packed light brown sugar, ½ cup whipping cream, and a pinch of salt. Cook and stir until blended over medium-low heat for 2 minutes. Increase heat and boil 2 minutes or until dime-size bubbles cover the surface of the glaze. Remove from heat and cool slightly, about 5 minutes, until glaze begins to thicken. Spoon over cake.

PER SERVING 568 **CAL**; 35 g **FAT** (7 g **SAT**); 61 mg **CHOL**; 256 mg **SODIUM**; 62 g **CARB**; 2 g **FIBER**; 5 g **PRO**

Rhubarb and Spice Snacking Cake

Mix up a pan of this extraeasy cake in early spring, when the rosy stalks of rhubarb sprout from the ground and its crinkly, elephantine leaves unfurl in the sun.

MAKES 9 servings **PREP** 25 minutes **BAKE** 30 minutes at 350°F **COOL** 30 minutes

- ⅓ **cup granulated sugar**
- ⅓ **cup chopped pecans**
- 1 **tablespoon butter, melted**
- 1 **teaspoon ground cinnamon**
- 1 **cup all-purpose flour**
- ½ **teaspoon baking soda**
- ¼ **teaspoon salt**
- ⅛ **teaspoon ground nutmeg**
- ¼ **cup butter**
- ¾ **cup packed brown sugar**
- 1 **egg**
- ⅓ **cup sour cream**
- 1 **cup chopped fresh rhubarb or frozen unsweetened rhubarb, thawed, drained, and chopped**
- ¼ **cup golden raisins**
- 1 **teaspoon finely shredded lemon peel**

1 Preheat oven to 350°F. Grease and flour a 3-quart rectangular baking pan; set aside. In a medium bowl combine granulated sugar, pecans, the 2 tablespoons melted butter, and 1 teaspoon of the cinnamon until crumbly; set aside. In another small bowl stir together flour, baking soda, the remaining 1 teaspoon cinnamon, the salt, and nutmeg; set aside.

2 In a medium mixing bowl beat the ½ cup butter with an electric mixer on medium to high for 30 seconds. Beat in brown sugar until well combined. Beat in eggs. Alternately add flour mixture and sour cream to butter mixture, beating until combined after each addition (batter will be thick). Stir in rhubarb, raisins, and lemon peel.

3 Spread mixture evenly in the baking pan. Sprinkle with crumb mixture. Bake for 30 to 35 minutes or until a wooden toothpick inserted near the center of cake comes out clean. Cool in pan on a wire rack for 30 minutes. Serve warm. Or cool completely and serve at room temperature.

PER SERVING 276 **CAL**; 12 g total **FAT** (6 g **SAT**); 45 mg **CHOL**; 223 mg **SODIUM**; 41 g **CARB**; 2 g **FIBER**; 3 g **PRO**

Warm Banana Bread Cobbler

Self-rising flour contains the baking powder and salt needed in this recipe. If you do not have self-rising flour, combine 1½ cups all-purpose flour, 2 teaspoons baking powder, and ¼ teaspoon salt to use in place of the 1½ cups total needed.

MAKES 12 servings **PREP** 20 minutes **BAKE** 25 minutes at 375°F **COOL** 30 minutes

1 cup self-rising flour
1 cup granulated sugar
¾ cup milk
½ cup butter, melted
1 teaspoon vanilla
4 medium bananas, peeled and sliced
1 cup rolled oats
¾ cup packed brown sugar
½ cup self-rising flour
½ cup butter
½ chopped walnuts
   Vanilla ice cream

1 Preheat oven to 375°F. Butter a 3-quart rectangular baking dish; set aside.

2 In a medium bowl stir together the 1 cup self-rising flour and the granulated sugar; add milk, melted butter, and vanilla. Stir until smooth. Spread evenly in the prepared baking dish. Top with sliced bananas.

3 In a large bowl combine oats, brown sugar, and ½ cup self-rising flour. Use a pastry cutter to cut in ½ cup butter until crumbly. Stir in walnuts. Sprinkle mixture over bananas. Bake for 25 to 30 minutes or until browned and set. Serve warm with vanilla ice cream.

PER SERVING 560 **CAL**; 28 g **FAT** (15 g **SAT**); 74 mg **CHOL**; 378 mg **SODIUM**; 75 g **CARB**; 3 g **FIBER**; 7 g **PRO**

Lovers' Pie

Although Mulberry, Florida, baker Jeanne Eli works full time and doesn't enter other contests very often, she never misses the American Pie Council's Great American Pie Festival. The festival, attended by nearly 39,000 pie lovers and featuring and "endless pie buffet," brings America's best pie bakers together in a delicious but intense competition. Each year for the last 10 years, Janet has entered 7 pies across different categories, taking home several wins. Her Lovers' Pie—entered in the Amateur Chocolate category, took First Prize honors in 2012, winning Jeanne, whose nickname is the Queen of Cream, the $500 prize.

MAKES 8 to 10 servings **PREP** 45 minutes **CHILL** 2 hours

1   **15.5-ounce package chocolate sandwich cookies with white filling, finely crushed (4 cups)**
⅔   **cup butter-flavor Crisco**
½   **cup margarine**
¾   **cup granulated sugar**
4   **ounces unsweetened chocolate, melted and cooled**
½   **cup refrigerated or frozen egg product, thawed**
1   **cup whipping cream**
½   **cup granulated sugar**
½   **cup lemon-lime carbonated beverage**
1   **tablespoon cornstarch**
½   **3-ounce package strawberry-flavored gelatin (3 tablespoons)**
½   **teaspoon lemon juice**
1   **pint fresh strawberries, hulled and halved**
¾   **cup whipping cream**
¼   **cup powdered sugar**
¼   **teaspoon vanilla bean paste or ¼ teaspoon vanilla**

1 For the crust, place the crushed cookies in a large bowl. Melt the butter-flavor Crisco; add slowly to crushed cookies. Press into a deep-dish 9-inch pie plate or a 9-inch heart-shape pie plate. Place crust in the refrigerator while preparing the filling.

2 For the filling, in a medium mixing bowl beat together the margarine and the ¾ cup granulated sugar. Stir in cooled chocolate. Add egg product, half at a time, beating for 5 minutes after each addition. In a large mixing bowl beat the 1 cup whipping cream with an electric mixer on high about 4 minutes or until stiff peaks form (tips stand straight). Fold the chocolate mixture into the whipped cream. Spoon into the pie plate, smoothing the top. Cover and chill until firm, about 1 hour.

3 For the topping, in a small saucepan combine the ½ cup granulated sugar, lemon-lime beverage, and cornstarch. Cook and stir over medium heat until mixture becomes clear and thickens. Stir in the strawberry gelatin and lemon juice; cool. Dip strawberries in the gelatin mixture and place on the set chocolate filling to cover. Spoon any remaining gelatin mixture over the strawberries.

4 For the garnish, in a medium mixing bowl combine the ¾ cup whipping cream, powdered sugar, and vanilla paste. Beat with an electric mixer on medium until soft peaks form (tips curl). Spoon into a pastry bag fitted with a large star tip. Pipe rosettes around the edge just inside the crust. Refrigerate until ready to serve.

PER SERVING 928 **CAL**; 66 g **FAT** (26 g **SAT**); 72 mg **CHOL**; 452 mg **SODIUM**; 88 g **CARB**; 5 g **FIBER**; 6 g **PRO**

Salted Caramel Apple Pie

This beauty is a true autumn indulgence. For fuller, more complex flavor, consider using more than one variety of apple in the pie.

MAKES 8 servings **PREP** 1 hour **BAKE** 50 minutes at 375°F

1   **recipe Oat Pastry**
¼   **cup all-purpose flour**
¼   **cup granulated sugar**
½   **teaspoon ground cinnamon**
2½   **pounds cooking apples, such as Fuji or Granny Smith, peeled and cut into ¼-inch slices (about 7 cups)**
1   **recipe Salted Caramel Sauce**
     Fleur de sel or sea salt (optional)
1   **egg, lightly beaten**
1   **tablespoon whipping cream**
     Coarse sugar

1 Prepare Oat Pastry. On a lightly floured surface use your hands to slightly flatten the larger pastry ball. Roll pastry from center to edges into a circle about 12 inches in diameter. Wrap pastry circle around the rolling pin. Unroll pastry into a 9-inch pie plate. Ease pastry into pie plate without stretching. Trim pastry even with pie plate rim; reserve pastry trimmings. Roll the smaller ball to ⅛- to ¼-inch thickness. Using a 1-inch round cutter, cut out 50 to 60 rounds; reserve pastry trimmings. Place pastry rounds on an ungreased baking sheet; cover and chill until needed.

2 Form the reserved pastry trimmings into about sixty ½-inch balls. Brush edge of pastry with water and gently press balls onto pastry edge to form a border.

3 In a large bowl stir together flour, granulated sugar, and cinnamon. Add apples; gently toss to coat. Layer about one-third of the apple mixture in pastry-lined pie plate. Drizzle with about 2 tablespoons of the Salted Caramel Sauce. Repeat layers twice. If desired, sprinkle lightly with fleur de sel.

4 Preheat oven to 375°F. In a small bowl combine egg and cream. Lightly brush edge of pastry with egg mixture. Randomly arrange pastry rounds on filling, overlapping slightly and brushing tops of rounds with egg mixture. Once filling is covered, lightly brush entire top of pie with egg mixture. Sprinkle with coarse sugar.

5 Cover edge of pie loosely with foil. Place pie on center oven rack. Line a baking sheet with foil; place on lower rack to catch drips. Bake for 30 minutes. Remove foil from pie. Bake for 20 to 35 minutes more or until pastry is golden and filling is bubbly. Transfer to a wire rack. Serve slightly warm or cooled. Serve with the remaining sauce.

Oat Pastry: In a large bowl stir together 2 cups all-purpose flour, ½ cup quick-cooking rolled oats, and 1 teaspoon salt. Using a pastry blender, cut in ⅓ cup butter, cut up, and ⅓ cup shortening until pieces are pea size. Sprinkle 1 tablespoon ice water over part of the flour mixture; gently toss with a fork. Push moistened pastry to the side of the bowl. Repeat moistening flour mixture, using 1 tablespoon ice water at a time, until all of the flour mixture is moistened (⅓ to ½ cup ice water total). Gather two-thirds of the pastry into a ball, kneading gently until it holds together. Repeat with the remaining one-third of the pastry.

Salted Caramel Sauce: In a medium saucepan combine one 14-ounce package vanilla caramels, unwrapped; ½ cup whipping cream; and 1 teaspoon fleur de sel or sea salt. Stir over medium-low heat until mixture is melted and smooth. Makes 1½ cups.

PER SERVING 642 **CAL**; 29 g **FAT** (16 g **SAT**); 70 mg **CHOL**; 683 mg **SODIUM**; 87 g **CARB**; 3 g **FIBER**; 8 g **PRO**

Toasted Coconut-Macadamia Cream Pie

When purchasing cream of coconut, check the label to make sure you are not choosing coconut milk. Cream of coconut is much thicker and richer and is usually found in liquor stores or in the liquor section of supermarkets.

MAKES 8 servings **PREP** 40 minutes **BAKE** 14 minutes at 450°F/15 minutes at 350°F **COOL** 1 hour **CHILL** 3 hours

3	eggs
1	recipe Pastry for Single-Crust Pie
⅓	cup finely chopped macadamia nuts
⅓	cup sugar
¼	cup cornstarch
¼	teaspoon salt
2	cups milk
¾	cup cream of coconut
2	tablespoons butter
1	cup flaked coconut, toasted (see note, page 9)
2½	teaspoons vanilla
¼	teaspoon cream of tartar
⅓	cup sugar
1	tablespoon flaked coconut
1	recipe Coconut Shards (optional)

1 Separate egg yolks from whites. Set egg yolks aside. In a large bowl let egg whites stand at room temperature for 30 minutes.

2 Preheat oven to 450°F. Prepare Pastry for Single-Crust Pie. On a lightly floured surface use your hands to slightly flatten pastry. Roll pastry from center to edges into a circle about 12 inches in diameter. Wrap pastry circle around the rolling pin. Unroll into a 9-inch pie plate. Ease pastry into pie plate without stretching. Trim pastry to ½ inch beyond edge of pie plate. Fold under extra pastry even with the plate edge. Crimp edge as desired. Press half the macadamia nuts onto bottom and sides of pastry. Generously prick bottom and sides of pastry with a fork. Line pastry with a double thickness of foil. Bake for 8 minutes. Remove foil. Bake for 6 to 8 minutes more or until golden. Cool on a wire rack. Reduce oven temperature to 350°F.

3 For filling, in a medium saucepan combine ⅓ cup sugar, the cornstarch, and salt. Stir in milk and cream of coconut. Cook and stir over medium heat until thickened and bubbly. Cook and stir for 2 minutes more. Remove from heat. Lightly beat egg yolks with a fork. Gradually stir about 1 cup of the hot milk mixture into the beaten egg yolks. Add yolk

mixture to saucepan. Cook and stir until bubbly. Cook and stir for 2 minutes more. Remove from heat. Stir in butter until melted. Stir in the 1 cup toasted coconut and 2 teaspoons of the vanilla. Cover and keep warm.

4 For meringue, add the remaining ½ teaspoon vanilla and cream of tartar to egg whites. Beat with an electric mixer on medium about 1 minute or until soft peaks form (tips curl). Gradually add ⅓ cup sugar, 1 tablespoon at a time, beating on high about 4 minutes or until stiff peaks form (tips stand straight) and sugar is dissolved (rub a small amount between two fingers; it should feel completely smooth).

5 Transfer warm filling to the prepared pastry shell. Immediately spread meringue evenly over warm filling; seal meringue to edge of pastry. Sprinkle with the remaining macadamia nuts and the 1 tablespoon coconut.

6 Bake about 15 minutes or until top is golden.

7 Cool on a wire rack for at least 1 hour. Cover and chill within 2 hours. Chill for 3 to 6 hours before serving. If desired, garnish with Coconut Shards.

Pastry for Single-Crust Pie: In a medium bowl stir together 1½ cups flour and ½ teaspoon salt. Using a pastry blender, cut in ¼ cup shortening and ¼ cup butter until pieces are pea size. Sprinkle 1 tablespoon ice water over part of the flour mixture; toss gently with a fork. Push moistened dough to side of bowl. Repeat with additional ice water, 1 tablespoon at a time, until all of the flour mixture is moistened. Gather mixture into a ball, kneading gently until it holds together.

PER SERVING 472 **CAL**; 30 g **FAT** (19 g **SAT**); 97 mg **CHOL**; 297 mg **SODIUM**; 44 g **CARB**; 2 g **FIBER**; 7 g **PRO**

Coconut Shards: Preheat oven to 350°F. With a vegetable peeler shave curls from the inside of 1 fresh coconut. Spread in a single layer in a shallow baking pan. Bake about 5 minutes or until light brown.

S'mores Ice Cream Pie

Freezer desserts—such as this dreamy one, with its three yummy variations—are a smart way to prepare for easy summer entertaining. Make one of each; pop them in the freezer and you'll be ready for anything!

MAKES 8 servings **PREP** 20 minutes **FREEZE** 4 hours **STAND** 10 minutes

- **2** pints chocolate ice cream, softened
- **1** cup miniature marshmallows
- **1** purchased graham cracker crumb pie shell or chocolate-flavored crumb pie shell
  Miniature marshmallows
  Hot fudge ice cream topping, warmed
  Whipped cream (optional)
  Chopped honey-roasted peanuts (optional)

1 In a large chilled bowl stir ice cream until softened but not melted. Stir in the 1 cup miniature marshmallows. Spoon ice cream into pie shell. Cover; freeze for 4 hours or until firm.

2 Let pie stand at room temperature for 10 to 15 minutes before slicing. To serve, sprinkle top with additional miniature marshmallows. Drizzle with warmed ice cream topping. If desired, top with whipped cream and chopped honey-roasted peanuts.

*Note: Brushing the crust with egg white and prebaking it makes it easier to cut and better tasting. Preheat oven to 375°F. Brush pie shell with a lightly beaten egg white, then bake for 5 minutes. Cool completely on a wire rack before filling.

PER SERVING 376 **CAL**; 16 g **FAT** (9 g **SAT**); 22 mg **CHOL**; 219 mg **SODIUM**; 54 g **CARB**; 1 g **FIBER**; 4 g **PRO**

Peppermint-Stick Ice Cream Pie: In a large chilled bowl stir 2 pints peppermint ice cream until softened but not melted. Spoon ice cream into a purchased chocolate-flavored crumb pie shell,* spreading evenly. Cover and freeze for at least 4 hours or until serving time. Let pie stand at room temperature for 10 to 15 minutes before slicing. Serve with warmed hot fudge ice cream topping. If desired, sprinkle with crushed peppermint candies.

PER SERVING 345 **CAL**; 15 g **FAT** (9 g **SAT**); 30 mg **CHOL**; 269 mg **SODIUM**, 47 g **CARB**; 0 g **FIBER**; 5 g **PRO**

Honey-Pistachio Tart

Honey caramelized pistachio nuts and small bits of mixed dried fruits nest in a light and flaky pastry. Another time, consider making the tart with macadamia nuts.

MAKES 8 to 12 servings **PREP** 30 minutes **BAKE** 35 minutes at 375°F

- ½ cup sugar
- ¼ cup honey
- ¼ cup water
- 1½ cups chopped pistachio nuts, toasted (see note, page 9)
- ½ cup mixed dried fruit bits
- ¼ cup orange juice
- 2 cups all-purpose flour
- ¼ teaspoon salt
- ⅔ cup shortening
- 1 egg
- ¼ cup cold water
- 1 egg yolk, lightly beaten
  Coarse sugar or granulated sugar

1 Preheat oven to 375°F. For filling, in a medium saucepan stir together sugar, honey, and ¼ cup water. Bring to boiling, stirring until sugar is dissolved. Reduce heat to medium-low. Gently simmer, uncovered, for 15 minutes or until a light caramel color, stirring occasionally. Stir in pistachios, fruit, and orange juice. Return to boiling; reduce heat. Simmer, uncovered, for 5 minutes or until filling is slightly thickened, stirring occasionally. Set aside.

2 For egg pastry, in a large bowl combine flour and salt. Using a pastry blender, cut in shortening until pieces are the size of small peas. In a small bowl whisk together the egg and the ¼ cup cold water. Add egg mixture to flour mixture. Using a fork, toss until dry ingredients are moistened. Divide pastry in half. Form each half into a ball.

3 Slightly flatten one ball of egg pastry into a rectangle. On a lightly floured surface roll dough to a 16 x 6-inch rectangle. Wrap around rolling pin. Unroll into a 13½ x 4-inch oblong tart pan with removable sides. Ease pastry into pan, pressing it up the fluted sides. Trim pastry even with top edge of pan. Spoon filling evenly into crust.

4 For top pastry, roll out remaining pastry ball to a 10-inch square. Using a pastry wheel, cut ½-inch-wide strips. Weave strips across top of filling. Press ends into rim of pan. Brush egg yolk on lattice top and sprinkle with coarse sugar.

5 Bake about 35 minutes or until top is golden. (If crust browns too quickly, cover with foil.) Cool in pan on a wire rack. Remove sides from pan.

PER SERVING 519 **CAL**; 28 g **FAT** (6 g **SAT**); 53 mg **CHOL**; 91 mg **SODIUM**; 59 g **CARB**; 3 g **FIBER**; 10 g **PRO**

Peach Crisp

Whenever you make this homey dessert—in summer, when peaches are fresh, or another time with frozen peaches—the enticing aroma of this crumble-topped treasure will fill your home.

MAKES 12 servings **PREP** 30 minutes **BAKE** 40 minutes at 375°F

- 8 cups ½-inch-thick fresh or frozen peach slices, peeled if desired
- ⅓ cup granulated sugar
- 3 tablespoons all-purpose flour
- 1 teaspoon ground cinnamon
- 2 tablespoons honey
- ¾ cup coarsely crushed graham crackers
- ¾ packed brown sugar
- ½ cup all-purpose flour
- ¼ rolled oats
- ¼ teaspoon ground cinnamon
- ½ cup butter, cut up
  Vanilla ice cream (optional)

1 Preheat oven to 375°F. Thaw peaches if frozen; do not drain. For filling, in a very large bowl stir together granulated sugar, the 3 tablespoons flour, and 1 teaspoon cinnamon. Add peaches; toss to coat. Spread in a 3-quart rectangular baking dish. Drizzle honey over peaches; set aside.

2 For topping, in a large bowl stir together crushed graham crackers, brown sugar, ½ cup flour, rolled oats, and ¼ teaspoon cinnamon. Using a pastry blender, cut in butter until mixture resembles coarse crumbs. Sprinkle topping evenly over the peach mixture.

3 Bake, uncovered, about 40 minutes or until topping is golden brown and filling is bubbly. Serve warm, if desired with vanilla ice cream.

PER SERVING 391 **CAL**; 16 g **FAT** (10 g **SAT**); 52 mg **CHOL**; 138 mg **SODIUM**, 59 g **CARB**; 3 g **FIBER**, 5 g **PRO**

Five-Spice Pear Pie Bars

When purchasing pears for these spicy, citrusy bars, remember that for baking, fruit that is still quite firm is best.

MAKES 32 servings **PREP** 40 minutes **BAKE** 45 minutes at 350°F

3 **cups all-purpose flour**
2 **tablespoons sugar**
½ **teaspoon salt**
½ **cup shortening**
½ **cup cold butter**
2 **egg yolks, beaten**
⅓ **cup milk**
   Water
6 **cups peeled, cored, and thinly sliced ripe pears (about 2¼ pounds)**
1 **cup sugar**
1 **cup crushed cornflakes**
1 **teaspoon five-spice powder**
1 **egg white, beaten**
1 **recipe Orange Icing**

1 For pastry, in a large bowl combine flour, the 2 tablespoons sugar, and the salt. Using a pastry blender, cut in shortening and butter until pieces are pea size.

2 In a small bowl whisk together egg yolks and milk. Gradually stir egg yolk mixture into flour mixture, tossing with a fork to moisten. Sprinkle 1 to 2 tablespoons water over the pastry, gently tossing until all is moistened. Gather pastry into a ball, kneading gently until it holds together. Divide pastry into two portions, making one portion slightly larger than the other. Wrap and chill until needed.

3 For filling, in an extra-large bowl combine pears, the 1 cup sugar, the cornflakes, and five-spice powder. Set aside.

4 Preheat oven to 350°F. On a lightly floured surface use your hands to pat the large portion of pastry onto the bottom of a 15 x 10 x 1-inch baking pan. Spoon filling evenly into pastry-lined pan.

5 Between two sheets of waxed paper roll the remaining pastry portion to a 15 x 10-inch rectangle. Carefully peel off top sheet of waxed paper. Invert rectangle, pastry side down, over the filling. Carefully peel off waxed paper. Using damp fingers, press edges of the two pastry rectangles together. Cut a few slits in the top pastry; brush lightly with egg white.

6 Bake for 45 to 50 minutes or until pastry is golden, fruit is tender, and filling is bubbly. Cool completely in pan on a wire rack.

7 Drizzle with Orange Icing. Let stand until icing is set. Cut into bars.

Orange Icing: In a medium bowl stir together 1½ cups powdered sugar, 1 teaspoon finely shredded orange peel, and ¼ teaspoon vanilla. Stir in 1 to 2 tablespoons pear nectar until icing reaches drizzling consistency.

PER SERVING 179 **CAL**; 6 g **FAT** (3 g **SAT**); 21 mg **CHOL**; 81 mg **SODIUM**; 29 g **CARB**; 1 g **FIBER**; 2 g **PRO**

Shortbread Brownies

These layered lovelies make quite an impression—and it's a very good impression indeed. Pictured on page 164.

MAKES 36 servings **PREP** 25 minutes
BAKE 45 minutes at 350°F

- 2½ **cups all-purpose flour**
- ⅓ **cup packed brown sugar**
- ¾ **cup butter**
- 1¼ **cups miniature semisweet chocolate pieces**
- 2 **cups granulated sugar**
- ¾ **cup unsweetened cocoa powder**
- 2¼ **teaspoons baking powder**
- 1 **teaspoon salt**
- 5 **eggs**
- ½ **cup butter, melted**
  Chocolate ice cream topping (optional)

1 Preheat oven to 350°F. Line a 3-quart rectangular baking pan with foil, extending foil over edges of pan; set aside. For crust, in a medium bowl stir together 1½ cups of the flour and the brown sugar. Cut in the ¾ cup butter until mixture resembles coarse crumbs. Stir in ½ cup of the chocolate pieces. Press dough evenly into the pan. Bake, uncovered, for 10 minutes.

2 Meanwhile, in a large bowl stir together granulated sugar, the remaining 1 cup flour, the cocoa powder, baking powder, and salt. Add eggs, the melted butter, and vanilla; beat by hand until smooth. Stir in the remaining ¾ cup chocolate pieces. Carefully spoon over crust in prepared pan, spreading evenly.

3 Bake, uncovered, for 35 minutes more. Cool in pan on a wire rack. Using edges of foil, lift brownies out of pan. Cut into bars. If desired, drizzle bars with chocolate ice cream topping.

PER SERVING 180 **CAL**; 9 g **FAT** (4 g **SAT**); 44 mg **CHOL**; 121 mg **SODIUM**; 23 g **CARB**; 1 g **FIBER**; 3 g **PRO**

Macaroon-Chocolate Bars

MAKES 48 servings **PREP** 40 minutes
BAKE 33 minutes at 350°F **CHILL** 30 minutes

- 2 **cups crushed chocolate sandwich cookies with white filling**
- ½ **cup sugar**
- ⅓ **cup unsweetened cocoa powder**
- ½ **cup butter, melted**
- 1 **teaspoon vanilla**
- ⅔ **cup all-purpose flour**
- ⅓ **cup sugar**
- ¼ **teaspoon salt**
- 2¾ **cups flaked coconut**
- 3 **egg whites, lightly beaten**
- ½ **teaspoon vanilla**
- ½ **cup semisweet chocolate pieces**
- 1 **teaspoon shortening**
  Whole almonds, toasted (see note, page 9) (optional)

1 Preheat oven to 350°F. Line a 13 x 9 x 2-inch baking pan with foil, extending the foil over edges of pan. Lightly grease foil; set pan aside.

2 For crust, in a large bowl stir together crushed cookies, ½ cup sugar, and cocoa powder. Stir in melted butter and 1 teaspoon vanilla. Press cookie mixture evenly onto the bottom of the prepared baking pan. Bake for 8 minutes.

3 In a large bowl stir together flour, ⅓ cup sugar, and salt. Stir in coconut. Stir in egg whites and ½ teaspoon vanilla until combined.

4 Spoon coconut mixture onto crust. Using wet hands, carefully press the coconut mixture to edges of pan. Bake for 25 to 28 minutes or until top is set and lightly browned. Cool in pan on a wire rack.

5 In a small saucepan cook and stir chocolate and shortening over low heat until melted. Drizzle melted chocolate over uncut bars. Chill about 30 minutes or until chocolate is set. Using the edges of the foil, lift uncut bars out of pan. Cut into 24 bars. Diagonally cut each bar in half to make 48 triangles. If desired, top each triangle with a whole almond.

PER SERVING 85 **CAL**; 5 g **FAT** (3 g **SAT**); 5 mg **CHOL**; 51 mg **SODIUM**; 10 g **CARB**; 1 g **FIBER**; 1 g **PRO**

MACAROON-CHOCOLATE BARS

Chocolate-Hazelnut-Caramel Thumbprint Cookies

These buttery-rich cocoa cookies filled with caramel and drizzled with chocolate are an interesting—and scrumptious— alternative to the more common jam-filled thumbprints.

MAKES 36 servings **PREP** 40 minutes **CHILL** 1 hour **BAKE** 10 minutes per batch at 350°F **COOL** 30 minutes

½ **cup butter, softened**
⅔ **cup sugar**
¼ **teaspoon salt**
1 **egg yolk**
2 **tablespoons milk**
1 **teaspoon vanilla**
1 **cup all-purpose flour**
⅓ **cup unsweetened Dutch-process cocoa powder**
1 **egg white, lightly beaten**
1 **cup finely chopped hazelnuts (filberts), toasted***
14 **individually wrapped vanilla caramels, unwrapped**
3 **tablespoons whipping cream**
½ **cup semisweet chocolate pieces**
1 **teaspoon shortening**
Toasted hazelnuts (filberts)*

1 In a medium mixing bowl beat butter with an electric mixer on medium to high for 30 seconds. Add sugar and salt; beat until combined. Beat in egg yolk, milk, and vanilla until combined. In a small bowl stir together flour and cocoa powder; beat into butter mixture until combined. Cover and chill for 1 hour.

2 Preheat oven to 350°F. Grease a cookie sheet; set aside. Shape dough into 1-inch balls. Dip in egg white; roll in the 1 cup hazelnuts. Place 1 inch apart on prepared cookie sheet. Make an indentation with your thumb in the center of each cookie. Bake for 10 to 12 minutes or until edges are firm.

3 While cookies bake, prepare caramel filling. In a small saucepan combine caramels and whipping cream. Cook over low heat, stirring frequently, until caramels are melted and mixture is smooth. After removing cookies from the oven, press cookie centers again, then fill with about 1 teaspoon filling. Transfer cookies to a wire rack to let cool.

4 In a small microwave-safe bowl combine chocolate pieces and shortening. Heat on high for 30 to 45 seconds or until softened; stir until smooth. Place a small mound of chocolate on each cookie. Top with a hazelnut. Let stand until chocolate is set.

***Note:** To toast hazelnuts, spread in a single layer in a shallow baking pan. Bake in a 350°F oven for 5 to 10 minutes or until light golden brown, watching carefully and stirring once or twice. To remove the papery skins from the hazelnuts, rub them with a clean dish towel.

PER SERVING 116 **CAL**; 7 g **FAT** (3 g **SAT**); 14 mg **CHOL**; 51 mg **SODIUM**; 12 g **CARB**; 1 g **FIBER**; 2 g **PRO**

Index

Metric Information

The charts on this page provide a guide for converting measurements from the U.S. customary system, which is used throughout this book, to the metric system.

PRODUCT DIFFERENCES

Most of the ingredients called for in the recipes in this book are available in most countries. However, some are known by different names. Here are some common American ingredients and their possible counterparts:

- Sugar (white) is granulated, fine granulated, or castor sugar.
- Confectioners' sugar is icing sugar.
- All-purpose flour is enriched, bleached or unbleached white household flour. When self-rising flour is used in place of all-purpose flour in a recipe that calls for leavening, omit the leavening agent (baking soda or baking powder) and salt.
- Light-color corn syrup is golden syrup.
- Cornstarch is cornflour.
- Baking soda is bicarbonate of soda.
- Vanilla or vanilla extract is vanilla essence.
- Green, red, or yellow sweet peppers are capsicums or bell peppers.
- Golden raisins are sultanas.

VOLUME AND WEIGHT

The United States traditionally uses cup measures for liquid and solid ingredients. The chart, top right, shows the approximate imperial and metric equivalents. If you are accustomed to weighing solid ingredients, the following approximate equivalents will be helpful.

- 1 cup butter, castor sugar, or rice = 8 ounces = ½ pound = 250 grams
- 1 cup flour = 4 ounces = ¼ pound = 125 grams
- 1 cup icing sugar = 5 ounces = 150 grams

Canadian and U.S. volume for a cup measure is 8 fluid ounces (237 ml), but the standard metric equivalent is 250 ml.

1 British imperial cup is 10 fluid ounces.

In Australia, 1 tablespoon equals 20 ml, and there are 4 teaspoons in the Australian tablespoon.

Spoon measures are used for smaller amounts of ingredients. Although the size of the tablespoon varies slightly in different countries, for practical purposes and for recipes in this book, a straight substitution is all that's necessary. Measurements made using cups or spoons always should be level unless stated otherwise.

COMMON WEIGHT RANGE REPLACEMENTS

Imperial / U.S.	Metric
½ ounce	15 g
1 ounce	25 g or 30 g
4 ounces (¼ pound)	115 g or 125 g
8 ounces (½ pound)	225 g or 250 g
16 ounces (1 pound)	450 g or 500 g
1¼ pounds	625 g
1½ pounds	750 g
2 pounds or 2¼ pounds	1,000 g or 1 Kg

OVEN TEMPERATURE EQUIVALENTS

Fahrenheit Setting	Celsius Setting*	Gas Setting
300°F	150°C	Gas Mark 2 (very low)
325°F	160°C	Gas Mark 3 (low)
350°F	180°C	Gas Mark 4 (moderate)
375°F	190°C	Gas Mark 5 (moderate)
400°F	200°C	Gas Mark 6 (hot)
425°F	220°C	Gas Mark 7 (hot)
450°F	230°C	Gas Mark 8 (very hot)
475°F	240°C	Gas Mark 9 (very hot)
500°F	260°C	Gas Mark 10 (extremely hot)
Broil	Broil	Grill

*Electric and gas ovens may be calibrated using celsius. However, for an electric oven, increase celsius setting 10 to 20 degrees when cooking above 160°C. For convection or forced air ovens (gas or electric) lower the temperature setting 25°F/10°C when cooking at all heat levels.

BAKING PAN SIZES

Imperial / U.S.	Metric
9x1½-inch round cake pan	22- or 23x4-cm (1.5 L)
9x1½-inch pie plate	22- or 23x4-cm (1 L)
8x8x2-inch square cake pan	20x5-cm (2 L)
9x9x2-inch square cake pan	22- or 23x4.5-cm (2.5 L)
11x7x1½-inch baking pan	28x17x4-cm (2 L)
2-quart rectangular baking pan	30x19x4.5-cm (3 L)
13x9x2-inch baking pan	34x22x4.5-cm (3.5 L)
15x10x1-inch jelly roll pan	40x25x2-cm
9x5x3-inch loaf pan	23x13x8-cm (2 L)
2-quart casserole	2 L

U.S. / STANDARD METRIC EQUIVALENTS

⅛ teaspoon = 0.5 ml	⅓ cup = 3 fluid ounces = 75 ml
¼ teaspoon = 1 ml	½ cup = 4 fluid ounces = 125 ml
½ teaspoon = 2 ml	⅔ cup = 5 fluid ounces = 150 ml
1 teaspoon = 5 ml	¾ cup = 6 fluid ounces = 175 ml
1 tablespoon = 15 ml	1 cup = 8 fluid ounces = 250 ml
2 tablespoons = 25 ml	2 cups = 1 pint = 500 ml
¼ cup = 2 fluid ounces = 50 ml	1 quart = 1 litre